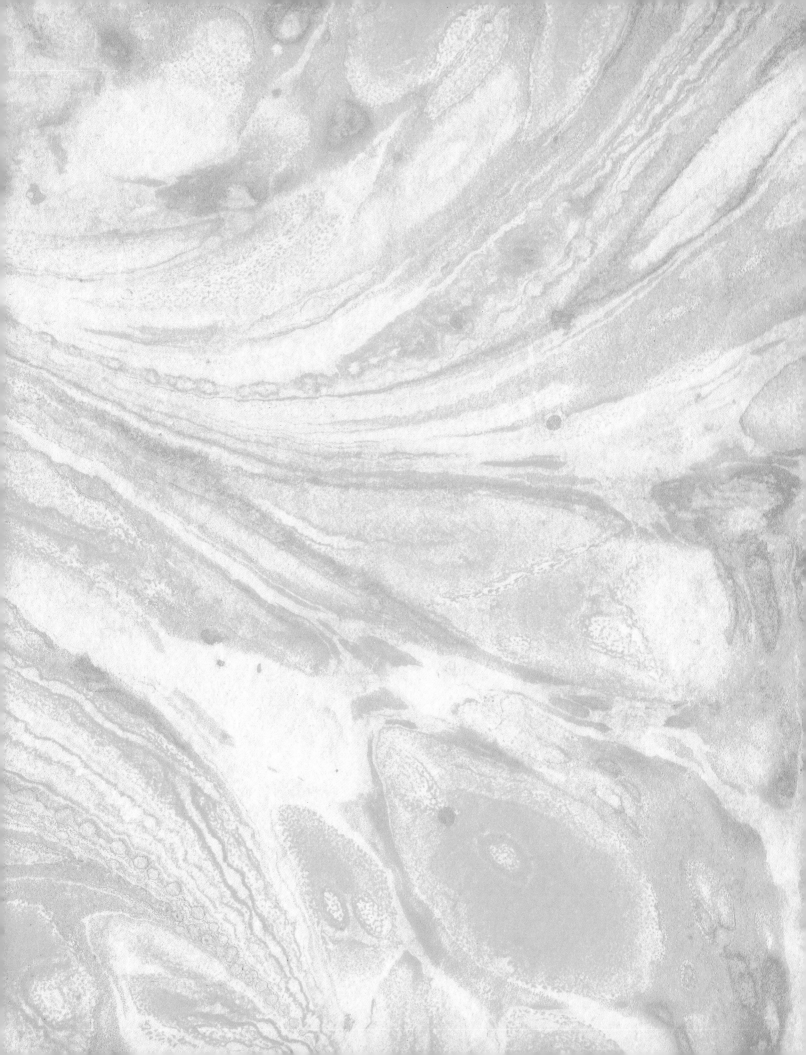

Celerie Kemble
TO YOUR TASTE

Celerie Kemble
TO YOUR TASTE

Creating Modern Rooms with a Traditional Twist

CELERIE KEMBLE WITH KAREN KELLY
PRINCIPAL PHOTOGRAPHY BY ZACH DESART
DESIGN BY DINA DELL'ARCIPRETE/dk DESIGN PARTNERS NYC

CLARKSON POTTER/PUBLISHERS
NEW YORK

Published in the United States by Clarkson
Potter/Publishers, an imprint of
the Crown Publishing Group, a division of
Random House, Inc., New York.
www.crownpublishing.com
www.clarksonpotter.com

Clarkson Potter is a trademark and Potter
with colophon is a registered
trademark of Random House, Inc.

Library of Congress Cataloging-in-Publication
Data is available on request.

ISBN 978-0-307-39442-2

Printed in China

10 9 8 7 6 5 4 3 2

First Edition

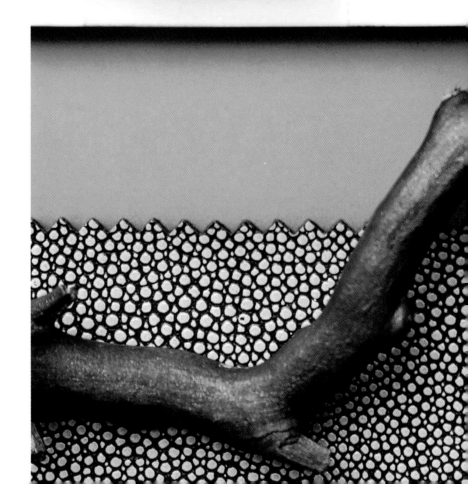

To the Old Bethesda-by-the-Sea Church, a graceful beauty, true character, and place that I love as one can only love home

CONTENTS

In a perfect world, we wouldn't need interior decorators. The citizenship would possess magical skills that could wrench mahogany from mud, silk from saccharine. But the world of interiors isn't perfect. Things fall apart. Chintz happens.

Decorators are essential.

This I first concluded some years ago when writing elsewhere about the late, great Sister Parish. You wouldn't pilot your own plane without a license, birth your own baby without some kind of primer, or lift your own face when you want to renovate, would you? And when we cannot swing decorators' budgets, we rely on books and shelter magazines, those merry, glossy gazettes that, almost Robin Hood style, bring us their richly useful news and how-tos.

Every generation gets the decorator it deserves; enter our friend Celerie Kemble. Creative but practical, glamorous but not affected, she is in the style trenches daily up to her BlackBerry in multitasking, turning empty spaces into lively 21st-century rooms. She is a powerhouse on a construction site, brilliant with a spreadsheet, a woman who lives and works as well as she looks, wife to one very special gentleman, devoted mother to two children, and boss to about a dozen young decorating stars.

Her mother, Mimi McMakin, founded the family's Kemble Interiors in Florida in 1986. After graduating Harvard, Celerie worked as a production manager in films, great training for decorating, she says, because "every house is a story line and every person is an epic." From movies she segued to opening Kemble Interiors' Manhattan office about ten years ago and has since become the modern personification of the savvy lady decorator, and from the manner, and manor, born (there are pictures of the manor in this book, just wait). This is very useful, especially for clients seeking their own stately pile, whether it is a penthouse aerie, rocking bachelor pad, fabulous loft, weekend house, glittering office, smart shop . . . well, you get the idea.

"If I wanted to live large, if I wanted that kind of lifestyle, I'd go straight to the source. . . . Wouldn't you rather have someone who grew up with beautifully appointed guest rooms?" the legendary Marian McEvoy, a contributing editor at *Domino,* told the *New York Times'* Penelope Green in a 2006 article that, among other topics, compared Celerie to—who else?—Sister Parish.

But there are some major distinctions. Back in the day, when it was a decorator's job to put together what polite society people used to call "a good house," very proper, very tidy, with important furniture and good rugs to sweep the unspoken under, Mrs. Parish, ever the "touchstone of the society interior . . . presented the decorator as autocrat, or at least a headmistress," Green wrote.

If Sister Parish and the few decorating peers she had were patrician and exclusive, and they were, then Celerie's generation is distinctly inclusive, inviting everything home—flea market, Christie's, doesn't matter, it is all the mix. Interiors then were representational rather than experiential. Nowadays, for Celerie, the goal is to design a space you want to live in, not that you should live in.

Big, sweeping, signature decorator statements are passé. As Celerie sees it, maybe it is the fashion world crossing over into the design world, but people have it as their prerogative to express themselves in their homes, to try things on.

(Spontaneity is one of the Kemble family's premium stocks. Consider how Celerie got her unusual name. On a sunny day some thirty years ago, in a conservative enclave in upper-upper New York State, mother Mimi was pregnant and wearing a bikini *sur le* lake. This shocked the older, lockjawed summer ladies, not inclined to seeing pregnant bellies or even bikinis. "Dear," one grand dowager announced, or words to this effect, "I do hope you won't be naming your child anything trendy like Cher or Chastity and will do her the favor of giving her a family name." To which Mimi, seeking some suitable, nose-thumbing retort, perhaps responding to the cheerful C in Cher and Chastity, or maybe it was the green stalk in the older lady's Bloody Mary that did it, declared on the spot: "My child will be called Celerie," and brava!)

As I saw firsthand at her wedding in 2005, where a chic, celebratory display of sentiment through design rendered any possibility of nuptial cliché impossible, Celerie's motivation in everything, from decorating to entertaining, is self-expression. Nonetheless, designing a home can be a very daunting and expensive process. Rich man, poor man, and everyone in between, no one ever has enough money. Everyone is always trying to stretch practicality and what they have to meet their dreams. No matter the scale, every Celerie Kemble project is an execution of spatial, financial, and personal compromises.

Whether for her clients or her book's readers, Celerie's mission, always, "is to help execute visions." She offers help, inspiration, and tips and shares secrets. She names sources and credits other decorators where credit is due. Here is the friendly, caring expert and coach you have wanted and needed—informative, instructional, and never dictatorial. Her message: If you know the rules, then you can redefine them and live "to your taste."

A Designing Life

Trying to clean up after a dismal 2 A.M. flight ordeal with my fourteen-month-old son, I hastily drew a lukewarm bath in the tiny tub of our grim motel bathroom. As I lay shivering in eight inches of water, squinting to block out the fluorescent lighting, and holding my sick, travel-weary baby, I was blinded by a sudden flash, and then heard laughter. My husband had snapped a picture of the two of us mid-soak, our flesh pale and shriveled against the margarine-colored plastic tub and shower curtain. He threatened to send the image to the editors at *Harper's Bazaar,* who had just published a particularly flattering photo spread that had me blushing with excitement when I saw it at the airport. In the magazine's photo (taken by their skilled photographer, my appearance carefully styled by a hair and makeup team), my son and I were luxuriating in a marble tub, garlanded with holiday greenery and illuminated with warm, subtle, radiant lighting. My husband thought *Harper's Bazaar* should run his motel snapshot alongside its glossy images under the respective headlines "Magazine Life" and "Real Life."

All of us have an idealized "magazine life" (the image we would like to project to the outside world, showing our best, most polished selves) and our "real life" (the often messy comfort zone where we raise children, eat microwaved meals, stretch out exhausted at the end of the day, and watch TV). A "magazine life" home is harder to achieve than a "real" one. Yet neither lifestyle is more authentic than the other—they are two sides of the same coin: how you'd like to live and how you actually live. The trick is to bridge the gap between the fantasies of what home should be like and the realities of our daily needs. No one wants a paint-by-numbers kind of home, where everything is contrived, like a condo showroom or a sterile hotel room; but who wants to live in stylistic anarchy?

Designing a home for both beauty and function fulfills two of our most basic needs. "We are the least expensive psychiatrists you can hire," my mother, the designer Mimi McMakin, says of our profession. The 20th-century American psychologist Abraham

> 66 There are as many styles of beauty
> as there are visions of happiness. 99
> —Stendhal

Maslow came up with something he called the "hierarchy" of human needs, which he regarded as essential for a happy, fulfilled life. Beyond the bare bones of air, water, food, and reproduction, he laid out a list of psychological essentials for survival, all of which also come into play when you are in the process of creating a successful room:

Safety and security (functional, sound rooms)
Love and belonging (rooms that welcome friends and family)
Esteem (rooms that make us feel and look good)
Self-actualization (rooms that reflect your personality and values)

There is no quick, straight path—the journey that brings you to a room that's ready for its close-up is long, winding, and unpredictable; we make up the map as we go. There are bound to be mishaps and mayhem along the way. I knew early on what I would be up against; I grew up in and around the design business. When my mother and I combine our stories with those of our design partners at Kemble Interiors, it turns out we've logged more decorating dustups than all of TLC's *Trading Spaces* shows put together. The job may sound glamorous, but the hands that choose the silver candlesticks definitely get a little grubby.

This brings me to a crucial point: in life as in design, it is not perfection you should be after. There's beauty in the faded and worn, the well loved, and the sentimental. Some critics disapproved of the famous Hollywood designer and former set decorator Tony Duquette's tendency to "let the seams show" in his rooms, but I love the way he celebrates the artifice of design and breaks the monotony of traditional style with relaxed whimsy and exuberant personality. After all, life has seams. Your home should be like a loosely woven fabric of desires, memories, practical notions, and even compromises. Living in it, you mold it to yourself; you are what holds it together and makes it beautiful.

Yet people are often afraid that their taste is wrong; they are fearful that the cost of making changes will be prohibitive; they are anxious about making expensive mistakes; and, more broadly, we are all busy—it often seems easier to put off the time-consuming task of reordering your home than to tackle it, even though you long to be surrounded by an environment that soothes and delights you. How do you determine the range of options that are available? Where do you go to find the best paint, fabric, upholstery, lamps, and art objects? How do you learn what goes together well? It can all seem daunting to someone who does not know the terrain. Armed with information, the right attitude, and the understanding that you are working toward the goal of beauty and comfort, these challenges, and others you confront, can be gracefully overcome. This is what I strive to create for my clients. It is also what I hope to share with you in this book.

I take my obligations to my clients, and to you, seriously: materials, furniture, and art are very expensive. At the end of a project, you, like my clients, should feel the result is a reflection of *your* ideas, standards, and preferences, not mine. In my professional life I try to familiarize myself with all the design possibilities that my clients would want to have in their own mental flip book as they enter into this process. Since you do not have me beside you, I have assembled inspiring images, along with many time-tested principles and guidelines, tips and ideas, to help you, whether you go it alone or enlist the help of an interior designer.

> ❝ I see a wild civility:
> Do more bewitch me than when art
> Is too precise in every part. ❞
> —Robert Herrick

You probably won't like every room you see in this book. That's all right; your own process of putting together a house should be informed as much by what you reject as by what you affirm. There is no right or wrong way; what's important is determining *your* way, and rejoicing when you find a space that speaks to you. In design, there may be ten ways to do something right, three that appeal to you, and one that reminds you who you are and what you would like to be. Use what is here to help you create a home that defines you, what you like, and how you live, color by color, and piece by piece.

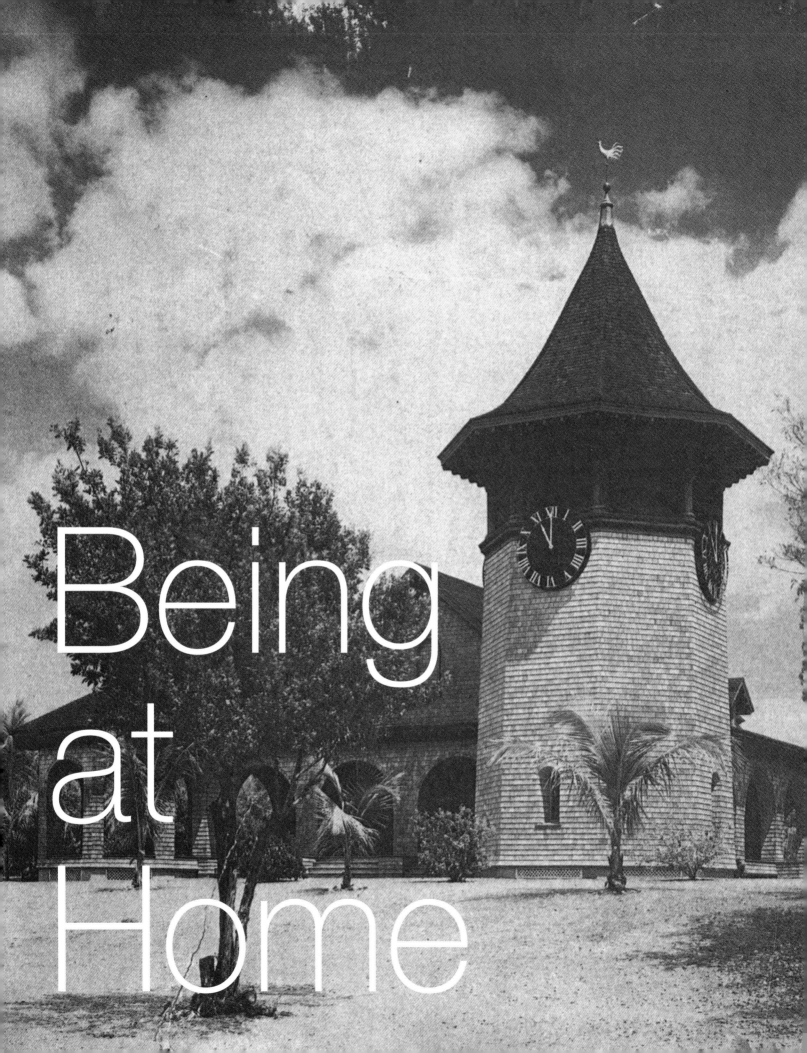

Being
at
Home

Chapter One

As a child, I roamed the airy, light-filled breezeways of my family home, sometimes on roller skates, often pursued by a pack of skittering dogs or cats—or whatever animals we'd let into the menagerie. I knew our household was an unusually joyous place, full of mayhem and life, but it wasn't until later that I realized how extraordinary the structure was in itself. Although it was built in the shingle style, like a summerhouse on Nantucket, it was shaped like a castle—complete with flying buttresses, 30-foot ceilings, a turret, and arched windows, some of them stained glass, many with a view through the crooked palm trees dotting the inter-coastal waterway that met the lawn's edge. Unlike many houses, it had its own name: "The Church of Bethesda-by-the-Sea." Before it became my family's house, in 1974, it had been an Episcopal church, serving the families that lived on our island, Palm Beach—the sunny resort community on the southeast coast of Florida.

My great-great-grandfather Henry Maddock built a house called Duck's Nest for his wife and gave the adjoining property to its south for the use of the church. My great-grandmother Lucile Lacoste Maddock was one of the women among the early settlers of the island who pushed for the creation of the church as we now know it. Her son, my grandfather Paul Maddock, built his house one lot south and bought all three properties to hold in family trust. Deconsecrated as a place of worship in 1925, it is now exalted in a different way, as our home. My mother, father, and stepfather have spent decades continuing to make sure the house is taken care of.

I start my story here, with the most magical house I've ever encountered. My passion for inte-rior design grew out of my experience of the powerful effect a physical space can have on our spirits, energy, outlook—even our personality. Where and how you live shape who you are. As an interior designer, my calling to help other people create their dream spaces comes from my desire to show them how to bring a sense of wonder, comfort, creativity, and belonging into their own lives as the Old Church did in mine.

I grew up in the house, but I also watched it develop, as my mother, designer Mimi McMakin of Kemble Interiors, transformed its surfaces to reflect her humor, grace, and good nature. The Old Church is almost a family member and is my muse for the inspirations I share with my clients. A century ago, Virginia Woolf wrote disparagingly of the "angel of the house"—the benevolent woman who sacrifices herself to enhance the happiness of others. But with the right design choices, nobody needs to martyr themselves in order to feel nurtured or to nur-ture others: the angel *is* the house.

Of course, as a child, I took its beauty and singularity for granted. I envied my friends' orderly Bermuda-style houses, with neatly manicured lawns. In stark contrast, an unruly Eden spilled out around my home—shaggy palms, topiary giraffes, fragrant clumps of gardenias popping out any which way, frilly trumpets of hibiscus blossoms emerging from a green tangle. Some of my friends' houses were quite grand (this *was* Palm Beach, after all), but what I coveted were the modern conveniences: clean-lined kitchens with spacious pantries, proper closets, a one-bath-per-bedroom layout, well-insulated walls, and soft wall-to-wall-carpeted floors. Not to mention central air. Our house, with its organically designed breezeways and high ceilings, and with Florida's balmy weather, usually didn't need central air, but as a kid, I sometimes felt I was missing something that every other kid I knew had.

OPPOSITE, CLOCKWISE
FROM TOP LEFT
An early 1900s postcard of Bethesda-by-the-Sea Church; a placard advertising the sale of my great-grandparents' home; my grandfather Paul Maddock bought his family home back at auction; wild-child fun in the front yard; an aerial view of Duck's Nest, the Old Church, and Tree Tops, three generations of houses side by side; a 1980s family portrait by John Haynesworth; the front of the Palm Beach Hotel; a postcard of the hotel; a photo of Mom, Dad, Phoebe, and me on the lawn in the 1980s, also taken by Haynesworth; Lucile Lacoste diving into the intercoastal waterway.

The gazebo my mother converted into a bedroom for me in the 1980s (nearly a century after it was built) had no closets and no bathroom. But oh, the light! And if we'd had wall-to-wall carpeting, how could I have roller-skated indoors? The Old Church was like a gorgeous vintage Jaguar that shuts down the first time the thermometer dips below 70, but that you can't help revering—a magnificent relic with beautiful lines, whose value transcends the practical.

Leaks were common, and we lost power almost weekly during late-summer afternoon rainstorms. Years passed before I realized that most people weren't accustomed to breaking out the candles every time there was a cloudburst. And yet I can't help thinking that the many nights we spent in half-darkness, reading by firelight, represent a link to our home's history as a place of worship. A church is built to inspire reverence, thankfulness, and awe, and to foster a sense of community, sharing, and peace. As a family home, the building evoked those same emotions for me and invested our everyday life with extra meaning and texture. The 14-foot ceilings, octagonal bedrooms, and 12-foot arched windows provided an exalted backdrop to our daily routine, and we had the constant hum of crickets and cicadas for a choir.

LEFT
Tame-for-ten-minutes family portrait on the lakefront porch, early 1970s.

OPPOSITE
An old postcard of the Bethesda-by-the-Sea Church; my great-grandparents Lucile Lacoste and Sydney Maddock in front of the Palm Beach Hotel.

Palm Beach, Fla. The Episcopal Church of Bethesda by the Sea, and Lake Front Drive, north.

OPPOSITE

Layers of memories, collections, family portraits, and relics keep time's continuum obscured in the Old Church. Here, a mix of photos from the 1970s to today shows details of our evolving home, including an old stage set backdrop from the early 1900s, a portrait of my stepfather's mother, and trompe l'oeil kitchen cabinets that immortalize pets of the past. An injured chicken that took several weeks' sanctuary in my father's bathroom is caught here gazing out a stained glass window.

FOLLOWING PAGES

The sitting room in the nave of the church, shown here in the 1990s, houses both treasures and detritus under flying buttresses.

To an outsider spying the house from the bike path along Lake Worth (neither my grandfather nor my mother felt right planting the tall ficus hedges that stand guard around most Palm Beach property), our house could suggest a haunted castle from a Charles Addams cartoon . . . albeit a sunny one plopped amid a jungle of overgrown foliage. Without question, our house was indebted to the South Florida landscape for much of its allure and mystique. Breezes floated through the rooms even when it was perfectly still outside. Adding to the *Alice in Wonderland* feel, families of foxes lived under the house (behind the trellises that hid its stilts) while opossums ranged through the wide lane of the double walls (nearly 2 feet separate the exterior and interior walls, insulating the house so it's cool in summer, warm in winter) and scuttled through the crawl spaces beneath them, their movements so familiar that the dogs would yawn while overhearing them, then fall back to sleep.

One year I listened to the entire life cycle of a brood of raccoons through the walls of my bedroom. Another time, a houseguest politely mentioned that several mornings running he had woken to find his hair and pillow mysteriously sticky. It turned out that a decades-old army of bees had filled the double wall behind his bed with a very productive hive. Honey had finally started seeping through the wall.

Some of the wildlife on the premises we brought in ourselves. My father kept a chicken coop in the backyard, inhabited not by the exotic, well-groomed hens you see in Martha Stewart's Easter tableaux, but by scraggly, belligerent birds who squawked all day long. My sister and I played complicated exploration and fantasy games. Hide-and-seek was out of the question. Once you hid, nobody could find you; and anyone looking for the hider was liable to get distracted. Tall palms swayed amid once-cultivated-but-long-since-run-wild pineapple plants and fruit trees—mango, papaya, avocado, star fruit, orange, grapefruit, key lime, tangerine, and kumquat. Gardenias and orchids grew so abundantly that you could fill wheelbarrows with the blooms, though they usually just dropped to the grass in a purple, pink, and white blanket. At night, after a hard day of play, I would drift asleep breathing in the scent of orange blossom that lingered in my hair.

As elaborate, graceful, evocative, and welcoming a structure as could be built at the time, the Old Church remains like a gracious hostess holding the door open with outstretched arms and an inviting smile that verges on a mischievous grin. It may sound as if I'm laying it on thick, but it's true. It's not unusual for strangers to walk right into the house, assuming it must be public property. And they're not really wrong. Strangers were free to look, form their own judgments, and even to come in and join us. My mother has always maintained an almost-open-door policy to anyone who has enough love and curiosity to wander in; she believes that our home is meant to be shared, and should therefore be open to passersby. And all the while, my mother never (and there is no exaggeration in the use of the word *never*) stopped adoring and adorning the house. One of her, and my, cardinal beliefs as a designer is that there are few greater joys than decorating your home to your satisfaction. Getting a new outfit revives your wardrobe. Bringing new design touches into your house renews your life.

For some fifteen years, whenever the late Brooke Astor was at her Palm Beach house, she would walk her dogs, Girlsie and Boysie, along the bike path that ran in front of our house. She would occasionally stop and rest in one of my mother's vintage-style groupings of outdoor

rattan furniture on the lawn. Every now and then, Mrs. Astor would ask to be served a glass of iced tea or water, thinking perhaps that she had arrived at some public park grounds with unusually inept café service. Once we picked up on it, one of us would rush to offer her a drink. At other times, tourists who apparently had been cooling their heels on the lawn would spot me descending the front steps in my school uniform and say with irritation, "We've been waiting out here for half an hour; when does the tour start?" More alarming, sometimes strangers would simply let themselves into the house, looking for public bathrooms—and surprise us while we were running around half dressed or sitting at breakfast in our PJs.

Everyone who enters the house feels a lift not simply because of its good bones and intrinsic spirit, but because it has been nourished for more than three decades by the deep well of my mother's love and design talent. It's the decoration and detail as much as the architecture that make the house so warm, happy, and magical. Without her care and her touch, the Old Church might be nothing more today than an aged building falling into ruin, something once grand but now outgrown and overgrown. But she has revived it and prolonged its life by filling it with sentiment and memory, whimsy, color, and character. Even if I sometimes yearned for a more conventional house like the ones my friends had, I was always impressed by my mother's commitment to making ours distinct. Because of my mother's passion and generosity, to this day, many of our friends and extended family members think of our house as part of their own traditions, a place to celebrate holidays and commemorate special occasions. Both my mother and I were married on its lawn. My mother twice!

Since going away to college in the 1990s, I've learned that I want to make wherever I live as much like home as possible, which leaves me with quite a task. The old Bethesda-by-the-Sea is impossible to copy. But the *feeling* of being surrounded by beauty, whim, and history is something that *can* be created.

In my life as a designer, the house and its surrounding land maintain a strong hold and influence over me. I am always working from the spirit of and connection to the decorative enthusiasm that surrounded me growing up. Since I began working as an interior designer a decade ago, it has been my mission to help my clients identify the beauty, whim, and history they want to incorporate into their own spaces and come to share my love for the design process. The process by which this alchemy is achieved has less to do with exacting standards or firm rules than with individual vision and ephemeral reach. Imagination is required! Because each client's undertaking is original and highly personalized, the process is intricate, but it's also rewarding. The point of all this is to surround yourself with a setting that satisfies your needs and delights your tastes and passions. It is important to keep the goal in sight.

I cannot remember a time when my mother was not working on improving our house, and showing me, through her example, how satisfying this work was. From the age of three or so, I accompanied her on her shopping excursions and decorating jobs, witnessing firsthand the many forms of fulfillment that come from good design. At her side, I also gained practical knowledge of the business end of her work—a world of sometimes demanding and always extraordinary clients, furniture makers, architects, seamstresses, and contractors. While other girls were playing with dolls and My Little Ponies, my playroom was the house itself, and the outdoors; my toys were paint chips, material samples, and wallpaper and fabric

swatches. Early on, design was demystified for me: it was fun, creative play that had wonderful, concrete results.

To people who come from families where interior design was not a priority, creating a personal style can seem daunting, or too demanding. This book will show you how to see the design process for all of its potential.

When I moved to New York City after college, my living situation was drastically different than it had been in Palm Beach. Manhattan can be an intimidating city that makes a newcomer, especially one on a small budget, feel like a bewildered and vulnerable bird kicked fresh from the warm nest. Months into my first job, after a long day working in what I had thought would be my dream career, film production, I returned home to an apartment that was still filled with moving boxes and the blank, unwelcoming stare of bald drywall. My occasionally shared minuscule sixth floor, one-and-a-half bedroom walk-up on Bedford Street in the West Village became a refuge in a city where I was of little consequence. I spent the next ten years nesting in and experimenting with my own first home.

Far from perfect, "home" had floors sloped so drastically that if you put a pool ball down on one end of the living room, it would roll across the surface and stop with a thump on the other end. It wasn't just slightly warped—there was a 4-inch difference in height between the front and back of the room. In winter, the cast-iron radiators would shudder in hissing, squealing, thunking spasms. Despite its drawbacks, however, the apartment was mine (insomuch as an affordable rental in New York City can be) and I loved foraging for furniture and accessories to decorate the little rooms. Gradually, I noticed that refurbishing my place was turning out to be more fun than working at the film company.

Wednesday in New York is the day when trash collectors pick up furniture and other oversized objects, so, with other like-minded scavengers, I would hit Dumpsters outside local apartment and office buildings midweek to sift through people's castoffs for goodies. On weekends I spent most of my time exploring the flea markets on 26th Street or window-shopping on Rollerblades for furniture in downtown vintage shops. Buying the Farm on Bond Street sported a sign with a cow belly-up. The Rural Collection on Perry Street brimmed with farm treasures from the Midwest and upstate New York. Both offered floor-to-ceiling inventory of old farm furniture with peeling paint (pie safes, cupboards, sideboards) and household objects (enamel jugs, picture frames made of reclaimed wood, milk glass, opaline and celluloid objects). It was the height of the shabby-chic era and I was living in a city short on country charm. There were other antiques stores that sold similarly countrified goods on Bond Street, including 30 Bond, Rhubarb, and, as I called it, Bob's "Small" Furniture Store (which had no sign, just an enormous sleeping rottweiler in front). Most of the other furniture stores on Bond Street were clearly part of the block family, each guarded by one of the pups of Bob's sleepy but sexually prolific guard dog.

One of the most important early influences on me was the now-closed Hope & Wilder on Broome Street, where chipped, scratched old dry sinks, enamel dishes, and hotel silver sat alongside vintage Swedish stemware and moss-covered terra-cotta planters. There I found mysterious cloudy steamed glass orbs called melon cloches, which farmers used to put in their fields to protect their melons. I turned one into a beautiful chandelier. Today, reproductions flood the market.

One of the store's owners, Michael Deperno, had an exceptional talent for finding and showing the inherent beauty in or unique aspects of the simplest objects. By setting vintage glass bowls, vivid in soft green and turquoise, against his store's subtle backdrop of creams and grays, he turned basic vessels into works of art. Celluloid shaving accessories, enamel hand mirrors and hat pins, and silver pillboxes so scuffed they seemed to emit their own hazy light were transformed into artifacts worthy of display in a cabinet of curiosities.

Though I could usually only afford to shop out of the bargain bin, no find was too large, odd, or inconvenient for me to drag home. Many hot summer evenings were spent hauling my treasures from Dumpsters and junking excursions back to Bedford Street. It was rare that I could persuade a taxi driver to employ his cab as a moving truck on my behalf. I'd usually end up walking, tugging along a massive trunk or three quarters of a daybed I planned to resurrect into a cozy napping nook—if I could only get it home.

My shoulders are still lopsided from dragging home two massive, unwieldy wooden stars (8 feet across, they had formerly adorned a barn) from the Hester Street flea market. I must have looked like some Wicca fanatic, transporting her magical paraphernalia to an occult ceremony, as I dragged them up Sixth Avenue. Once safely back in my apartment, I cleared half the furniture out of my living room so I could coat them with red floor stain. The stars found a home on opposite walls in the living room, then spent time in the kitchen, then landed in the middle of the bedroom and living room ceilings before going on indefinite loan to a friend.

Other items proved too heavy for my lugging ability, so I enlisted help. My boyfriend at the time (aptly named Tor, as in "tower") never complained about hauling my oversized loot, even when I suggested we tie an armoire (covered in peeling buttercream paint) to his back. Up the six flights of my building he went, Ben-Hur style.

I soon developed such a passion for shopping that if anyone wanted something for her apartment, I would volunteer to scavenge on her behalf. When the independent film production office I worked in needed furniture, I found 1930s enamel-topped splatterware kitchen islands to use as desks. After cutting down their legs, I lacquered them fire-engine red. They were totally impractical (no drawers or filing space), but they looked terrific. That was my Magnolia Bakery–meets–fire-station-in-the-West-Village–chic moment. As I slowly realized that I was more excited by my furniture discoveries than by the hurdles I was leaping in my day job, I began to wonder if I could harness my passion for decorating and turn it into my career. I decided to move back to Florida to work under one of the designers in my mom's firm, Kemble Interiors, and to see if interior design was really for me.

At the age of twenty-two, I already had a taste for vivid, rich hues, complemented by the soft patina of natural finishes, and had begun to explore the potential of repurposed objects. A decade of experience in design has deepened my confidence and broadened my sense of creative possibilities, but the fundamental aesthetic remains. I notice that my original eclectic approach and color preferences continue to come through in the choices I make with clients today—even though my design philosophy is more cohesive and considered, and the budget and spaces my clients work with are on a different planet from my own early circumstances. Your tastes have undoubtedly changed over time as well, and they will surely continue to do so. It's natural and exciting to build on old ideas as new ones inspire and captivate you.

OPPOSITE
From vintage shops such as Hope and Wider, to experimenting in my own tiny space, to watching magnificent design unfold in the hands of Brooke Huttig and Mimi McMakin in Palm Beach, my interior design vernacular evolves.

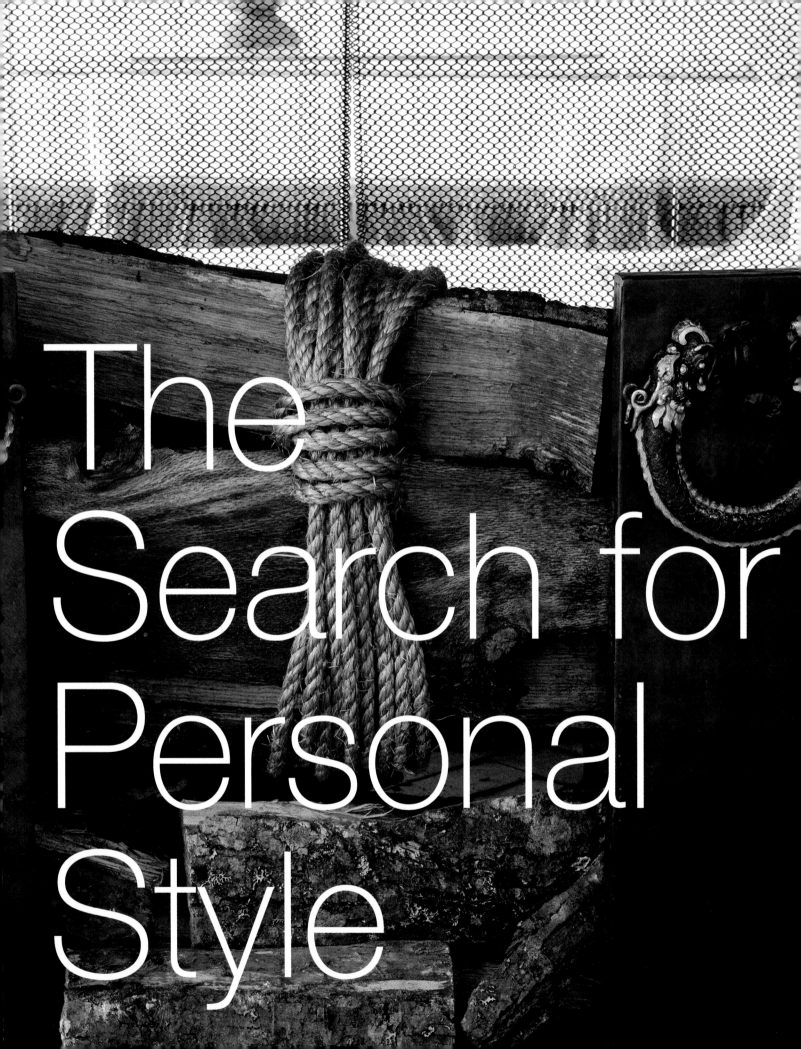

The Search for Personal Style

Delving into your own history is the first step in creating a space you want to live in—even if you end up defining what you love now as the opposite of what you grew up with. Some people consider their childhood home as something to return to and some as something to move away from. Either way, thinking about your beginning influences is still the starting point. What makes you feel natural and comfortable? Just as reviewing your medical history gives you clues to your future health, examining what you grew up with and how you felt about your environment may suggest how predisposed you are to clutter, formality, simplicity, color, or neutrality. It also provides you with a sense of what you will find easy to live with and what you will define as beautiful.

It's not unusual for clients to show me pictures of their childhood homes or even take me to visit them as we begin the decorating process. One client thought I would understand the quality she wanted in her home if she showed me her mother's current décor (lined and interlined curtains, glazed walls *and* moldings, high-crowned down seat cushions), making sure to point out details that she did not want in her own space (balloon shades, knickknacks, large vases below console tables, sculptures above).

Another client wanted me to duplicate the feel of his childhood home in his small apartment. After the death of his parents, he and his sister inherited their parents' apartment and everything in it. Although they decided to sell the apartment, as it was too large for the needs of either of them, he wanted to transfer as much of its spirit and style as possible to his own place. His parents' taste was distinctive, and their family apartment had a mix of antiques and

Design is the process by which imagination and memory become reality.

OPPOSITE

The modern industrial design in one client's mother's guesthouse informs her own selections, shown on page 35.

BELOW

From a massive apartment on upper Fifth Avenue to Greenwich Village, an apartment decorated entirely with design elements from a client's childhood home consolidates and protects family memories.

iconic elements of the Billy Baldwin/David Hicks design era. To initiate my client's design plan, I helped him sort and edit their possessions. We then moved a short list of furniture out of his parents' six-bedroom apartment on upper Fifth Avenue to his one-bedroom much farther down Fifth Avenue, in Greenwich Village.

The guiding principle of our approach was "use what you have." We applied careful spatial planning to include as many cherished pieces as we could fit into his apartment, while keeping in mind that he also wanted to create a feeling that would reflect his age, twenty-five, and his lifestyle. Once we had winnowed down the pieces, we took some other steps to make his place comfortable, homey, and fresh: we introduced a sleeper sofa into his study/TV room/ guest room; added built-in bookcases, new upholstery, and wallpaper; and created a bedroom décor scheme that matched the young man he was, rather than the formal aesthetic that his

parents favored or the preteen he had been when his room in the family apartment was originally decorated.

Not everyone could make such a literal translation of their childhood home and memories, or
would want to; but to gain a more definite sense of your style identity, it often helps to reflect
on where you came from. The recollection of a favorite chair or a private place where you used
to hide away from siblings, curled up with a book or listening to music, can remind you of features you would like to integrate into your new home. When a client reminisces about cozy
spaces or crowded kitchens, calming work areas or a central roaring fireplace where his family used to gather, those memories become information—hints a designer can use to generate
a house that feels like home. In decorating terms at least, show me where you were and I will
help you figure out who you are.

Rooms as Self-Definition

Our home can truly be a self-portrait—defining us for others, and reminding us of who we are.
The personal identity I try to bring out in every design project arises from the home owner's
expression of his or her priorities. It doesn't scare me when a client's likes and dislikes seem
to conflict, or when a multiplicity of priorities—sentiment, practicality, indulgence, or entertaining (for example)—makes the job tricky. It's only natural for a home environment to be as
complicated and multifaceted as its owner.

Personal history provides the framework, which we then embellish by mixing in a variety of
styles to create something unique. When I work with a client, we dip into any number of periods to achieve a space that makes sense for them. Like my mother, I believe that mixing styles
and periods and textures is not only the most beautiful way to adorn a room, but also the most
fun and flexible. If you deviate from a room that is purely nineteenth century or all modern,
you upset the applecart. But if the room blends the whimsy, adornment, grace, and movement
of, say, Chinese Chippendale, art deco, and 1940s French modern, you can add touches from
other vernaculars more freely. All these periods feel current together, because beautiful pieces
from these eras share elements of the sensuous, glamorous, and indulgent.

The best rooms come together with a subtle sleight of hand. An eye for detail, nuance, and
drama is joined with *discipline* to create a room in which an artful mix of disparate items play
off one another. Just as your closet is not confined to clothes for work, or play, or dress-up,
you don't want a house that's set up only for cocktail parties or only for private relaxation. But
there's a big difference between your closet and your home. A closet stores all the varying elements of a wardrobe discreetly behind closed doors. In your home, the different facets and
needs of your life exist out in the open for anyone to see. They should look cohesive—to
reflect the complex life you lead and the kind of person you are, without being a jumbled,
cacophonous mess.

OPPOSITE
*The living room and master
bedroom of a Tribeca
apartment (above, left and
right) reflect the textures
and interest in mid-century
design and rough-hewn
industrial elements of her
mother's home, below (which
was designed by Emily
Summers).*

FOLLOWING PAGES
*A New York–based client of
mine who grew up in Palm
Beach wanted to bring the
levity and celadon, rasp-
berry, cream, and aqua
palette of her family home
with her, which keeps her
living room airy and floral.*

It's About You, Not Your House

The most important element of any design scheme is the *person* who will inhabit the space, not the architecture of its walls. Some of the most memorable and lovely rooms I've seen flagrantly disregard their architectural frame. For example, a modern apartment done up beautifully with traditional décor, an American farmhouse detailed with Danish Modern furniture, and a spare glass-and-brick Tribeca loft filled with Louis XVI pieces. The bones of your house can be something to work with or against. Architecture is not what directs most residential design styles— unless the building is historically significant or highly stylized, such as an ornate Victorian house filled with hand-carved woodwork and stained glass, or a Frank Lloyd Wright "prairie house." Even the most thematic houses allow some breathing room for design discretion. Don't forget, the original owner of a 1892 or 1950s showpiece building was rarely a slave to the day's fashions. Why should you be forced to re-create them? Be emboldened to take a risk and work with your contractor, architect, and/or designer to add or subtract elements as you wish. This holds especially true in vacation homes, which are meant to reflect more fantastical facets of your life.

Even if you know art deco from art nouveau, can appreciate the undulating flair of a French chair leg, and feel confident holding forth on the relative merits of sculptures in a gallery, you may still feel challenged putting your artistic sensibility on display in your home. The most experienced designers often find starting from scratch a daunting prospect. But patience and a methodical approach can help you gain confidence in your decisions as you work toward a design that suits your taste, your budget, and your life.

OPPOSITE

Both of these clients came to me asking for modern rooms and even chose a similar palette, but their needs, circumstances, and selection of artwork and antiques resulted in two very different spaces.

Creative Consultation

The help of a good designer makes finding your style easier, but if you are going it alone, here's some advice: don't rush. If you are getting ready for guests or the holidays, a good cleaning is more effective than trying to completely redo your décor. Rooms are difficult to create "overnight" because the process of merging your particular needs and impulses with an aesthetic that will hold up over the years deserves careful consideration. Even in the hands of an expert, the best-designed houses evolve over time. First you need to come to terms with what does and doesn't work about your space. Then you can start to ask yourself what you would like to change and begin weighing likes and dislikes. Sourcing tends to be the next great challenge.

A successful scheme integrates important existing design elements and new possibilities. What we remember about someone's home is usually related to our sense of comfort or discomfort in it, our reactions to its color and material selections, and then the personal touches that make it theirs and theirs alone. When embarking on a design project, even a smallish one, begin by asking yourself these questions:

- How do you usually express yourself? With colorful anecdote or with careful, measured example?

- How long do you expect your choices to last? When do you expect your major pieces to reach stylistic obsolescence? How many years must something hold up and hold your love?

- How long will you be in the space you are thinking of reworking?

- Are you trend conscious, oblivious, or contrarian? Conservative, traditional, or laissez-faire?

- Do you want a formal, high-style home? Do you have a ramen-noodle dinner budget?

- Do you love French provincial armoires *and* mid-century modern sofas? Can you, *should you,* live with these disparate pieces in the same house, let alone the same room?

- What do you already own that you can't or won't part with? Why?

- How much time do you spend in each room, and what do you *really* do there?

- Who else has needs that must be considered? You may want to think ahead to consider the demands of future spouses or children (more closet space, another bathroom).

OPPOSITE AND RIGHT
*Two different rooms express
the needs and interests of their
owners. Both use cream, beige,
and black to set the color
scheme, but one reads
mid-century clean and the
other, with its red accents and
Colonial eclectic pieces, has a
very different personality.*

It is crucial to plot out your real-life routines and your design priorities well before you start to acquire. Consider how you really live instead of how you feel you should be living. You may fantasize about hosting dinners for twelve in a grand dining room but have spent the last decade eating out every night. Think twice before you commit funds and square footage to improbable use.

Apologia

I want to be open about what I do, and put it in a larger social context. Interior design is an indulgence, and one that can be very expensive. An appreciation of nice things is an icing-on-the-cake concern. It seems grossly presumptuous when designers casually discuss as "affordable" prices that most reasonable people consider ridiculous. On the other hand, I do what I do as a business, one in which I take great pleasure. In the expensive and sometimes demanding process of helping people create their dream personal spaces, I work with craftsmen and other skilled workers. Their commissions help keep alive the traditions of craftsmanship and art in addition to supporting a web of families.

In the weeks following September 11, 2001, I felt a piercing sense of emptiness as I wandered around the New York Design Center looking for coordinating fabrics for a client who was pushing me to complete my work before a November dinner party. What I perceived at the time as unnecessary drama about an artificially imposed deadline and the trifling concerns of a spoiled woman was the core responsibil-

ity of a collaborative design consultant's job—to respond to my clients' needs. It wasn't until months later that I decided I was lucky to be involved in the work of making people happy, even if it was on the level of stylistic indulgence. In the sunshine of this later mood, I saw that my client's urgency came from her desire to create a beautiful new dining room to share with her family in time for Thanksgiving.

Catering to the whims of some big-budget clients calls for frequent reality checks. I once met a designer (who later opted out of the business) who put our field in proper perspective. He told me about a client of his who was enraged when he wouldn't give her his cell phone number in case she had to call during a design crisis. He told her, "There is no such thing as a design emergency" and was promptly fired. Yet I understand the desire to make your home the most satisfying and flattering embodiment of the life and culture you live. More than mere shelter, your home is the backdrop of your life, and I think it's worth finding the time, the energy, and the means to make it special. Without apology.

A comfortable home should accommodate or facilitate your habits. Even the most traditional or formal rooms can be highly functional and sturdy, depending on what kinds of fabrics and finishes are chosen. So now, more questions—and suggestions about what direction a room should take:

- What do you do when you get up in the morning? How do you get ready for the day? If you like to dawdle and luxuriate, will it be in the tub or the shower? Do you want to sit or stand when you have a hair dryer in hand or as you apply makeup? If you are up and out in an instant, the bathroom really has to function at a high level—a no-nonsense, efficient style and floor plan are in order. If bathroom time is contemplation time, a bigger room with boudoir touches (a chaise lounge or a soaking tub, for example) might be the way to go.

- What happens when you come home? How and where do you like to wind down? This is where to focus your design dollars—where you spend your time.

- Do you read in bed, in a chair, or on the sofa? This will guide your decisions about lighting in each of these locations, and about how comfortable they must be for certain durations.

- Are you a wanderer, like me, pacing your house, coffee mug attached firmly to fist? Or do you sit down at a table? If you're short on space, is a dining table a necessity?

- What do you eat and where? Kitchen, dining table, coffee table? What feels right to you—a glass, stone, or wood top for these surfaces? Do you use a tablecloth?

- Do you eat out, cook, or order in? The kitchen can be rudimentary, streamlined, and small or a sprawling high-tech laboratory with accommodating places to eat in.

- When you entertain, do you vary your settings thematically? Are these items rented or expected to be standing by in a cabinet somewhere? For how many guests or family members must you store provisions and tableware?

- Where do you draw the line between chips, stains, and patina? Are you more comfortable with new or dilapidated?

- Do you read the newspaper for your news (smudges!) or watch it on TV? TV watchers need not be as concerned about fabric durability as newspaper readers unless meals and TV occur together.

- What is your cootie quotient? How raw, rugged, and abused can your vintage pieces be? Are you comfortable with the idea of previously owned furniture, fabrics, and rugs?

- Does mess give you stress? If you are focused on order, you may need to hold the line early on with fewer furnishings or finishes in durable materials so they maintain their new appearance. Dark-wood floors show scratches, footprints, and dust; light floors show scuffs, so stick with a medium tone or prepare to be driven to distraction.

- When relaxing in the living room, are you most often lying down or sitting? Where do you like your feet to rest? On the floor? On the sofa? On an ottoman? On the coffee table?

- Where do you sit to tie your shoes? Maybe you need a sofa in your bedroom, or an upholstered bench in the entryway.

Consider how you really live instead of how you feel you should be living.

LEFT AND BELOW
The sixty-eighth-floor midtown apartment draws its influence from the sky and surrounding buildings outside. While its bachelor owner desired modern and clean lines, he also wanted rich, warm textures and sensuously shaped furniture.

- Should every room be kid friendly? Do you care if the furniture gets nicked? It is not necessary to turn the place into a nursery school, or to pad the entire house to protect the child or furniture; it's better in the long run (for child and house) to teach a child to live in the house.

- How long can you keep a pair of white pants clean? (For me, it's about three hours.) That gives you a clue to the kind of fabrics you should buy—durable and washable or delicate and demanding.

- Shoes off or shoes on when you come in the door? If no one is ever going to walk in your house in shoes, you can expect to maintain a certain level of vigilant cleanliness. It's your responsibility to guard the materials you choose. The shoes-off person can have a white rug in the bedroom. My coffee mug and I can't.

What is the experience you want for each room? Check all that apply. . . .

_ Airy	_ Engaging	_ Minimal	_ Social
_ Calm	_ Exciting	_ Personal	_ Spacious
_ Casual	_ Formal	_ Relaxing	_ Spare
_ Controlled	_ Functional	_ Restful	_ Symmetrical
_ Conversational	_ Highly designed	_ Robust	_ Tidy
_ Cozy	_ Invigorating	_ Sensuous	_ Touchable
_ Efficient	_ Light	_ Serious	_ Witty
_ Energetic	_ Lively	_ Snug	_ Zen
	_ Meditative		

The Room in Your Head

Once you've established the style, personality, and amount of wear and tear a room will receive, you can formulate a design, look for inspiration, and shop. Take along the results of your personality quiz and your magazine clippings. Keep them in a little book tucked inside your bag for easy reference, along with tiny swatches of any existing paint or fabric colors and photos of your room—you never know when you may run across a seemingly perfect fabric and need your notes or a snapshot to check how well it really fits in with the scheme you've been developing.

When you are ready to shop, start small—as in save the sofa for last! Many people believe they need a sofa first, and can't think about fabrics, colors, end tables, lamps, or mirrors until after buying it. Allowing a sofa to determine a room's style and color scheme creates myriad design mistakes, because it's sort of the potato of the room. You don't know whether it should be baked, fried, whipped, or au gratin until you have the other food on the plate planned. The potato supports the meal, but it's rarely the star. If you plop it down in the middle, you're forced to work around and accommodate it. Forget about the sofa for the moment—you'll be able to find a good variety in sectionals, couches, and love seats when the time is right. Instead, consider the mood of the room first, then texture, color, and other details.

I advise you to begin the process with fabric and color selection. Look for a textile with a print or geometric that embraces the style you've honed in on, one that contains the colors you would like to see throughout the room (see Chapter 3 on color and texture). Establishing the colors and fabrics that will be used in a room makes it easier to select the material, finish, and color of the coffee table and side tables: wood, lacquer, mirror, skirted, or stone. Pick out the right versions of neutrals from your fabric or photo— creams, whites, beiges, grays, or browns—and use them for the elements you need a lot of, such as the ceiling color, large upholstery pieces (including the couch), flooring or rug color, and curtains. Use the other coordinating colors from your fabric or picture as smaller-scale accents, such as chairs, pillows, table skirts, ceramic or glass objects, or a piece of lacquered furniture. Accessories, small upholstery items (like chairs and ottomans), and smaller case pieces (end tables, consoles, and coffee tables) are going to carry the stylistic flag in the room, so look for them first. Sometimes a find on the street or a score in a junk shop embodies the idea (color, form, era) you have for the room and allows you to build out a room from that piece. In my experience, a room built around something unique tends to make more of a statement.

Don't Be Afraid to Fall in Love

If you are embarking on a project by yourself, and you fall in love with a particular object—a beautiful standing lamp, a sinuously shaped mirror, a seaworthy steamer trunk, whatever gets you giddy—*buy it*, regardless of whether or not you know how the room is going to take shape. Something one-of-a-kind and special helps determine the character of a room. People think it's dangerous to pull the trigger without knowing the whole plan, but sometimes the first impulsive purchase is a cornerstone that gives you direction. If you are on the fence, consider how adaptable it is by trying to imagine it in at least two rooms or two ways you might use it.

LEFT
Earnest elements such as mattress ticking for shades, a weathered wood table, wheat-back chairs, and Emma Bridgewater earthenware, all in a muted palette, give hearty simplicity to this country house dining room—and provide a warm and quiet backdrop for good conversation and wine drinking.

OPPOSITE
This room is vibrant, made to please a lively personality; highly saturated colors, luxe textures, chinoiserie accessories, ceramic fish lamp tables, blown glass, cut velvet, and antique rugs add up to a room with decadent glamour and whimsy.

IN THE HAMPTONS
A ROOM COMES TOGETHER

To give you an example of how a space is created once the consultation is over, let's start with the living room I designed for a family's weekend retreat in New York's Hamptons, a beach community on the southeastern end of Long Island, famed for its magnificent ocean vistas and extraordinary homes. In this case the house is a design show house, and the owners are in my imagination.

The Client

I see the family who owns this house as one with refined but not rigid tastes. They have traveled widely, love to entertain and welcome overnight guests, and, despite their sophistication, never stand on ceremony. This is the couple's second or third residence. Their two children are old enough to sit anywhere and invite friends to stay. This is not a "careful don't touch" couple. Most everything is new or vintage in the house except for accessories, which may have more provenance. A modern couple with contemporary tastes may nonetheless have somewhat old-school values—they like traditional scale and comfort, and enjoy both color and pattern. And it's the Hamptons, a place where they go to relax and have fun. That means seating is more plentiful, with a comfy sofa and an assortment of welcoming chairs that could be easily moved around and grouped according to occasion. That also means the tables used must stand up to drinks and feet and food.

The Parameters

We really had only one restriction in the large room: the crisp white molding and wainscoting could not be painted. Such limitations are not uncommon; there are usually some nonnegotiable items, even when you are decorating for yourself. In this case, the color of the trim meant I needed to find a wallpaper or fabric for the walls that contained a true white, so it would not fight the very dominant woodwork or—worse—look dirty next to the existing crisp white. I chose Animaux Warp Print in blond and pewter by Brunschwig & Fils. The fabric is a fresh fauna-and-flora print, slightly whimsical but not loud and not too literal. A coordinating fabric with a squirt of gray was needed to bring a bit of gravitas to the overall palette. I found hundreds: silks, velvets, cottons, linens, woven grasses, and leathers.

A flinty metallic faux leather went on the ottoman only because a real or faux leather chair would be a bit *too* serious (and maybe sticky on a warm summer day) for a beach house. And, as we were using a "leather" on an ottoman, I had to make sure it would hold up to wet bathing suits and the heat of the fire. I did not want a dark or heavy room, so I also felt it was important to pick up the yellow on the walls elsewhere. I decided to bring some sunshine to the sofa, which also had to be comfortable, relaxed, and durable. Velvet and mohair, traditional

sofa choices, seemed hot and scratchy, though I did seek their heft and durability. I would love to have used linen, but it was planned for the curtains, club chair, and coffee table, and I didn't want the room to be overoutfitted in the same texture. Chenille is a textile I try to avoid; it became so ubiquitous in the 1980s and 1990s, and I find its texture sort of dish-raggy. I kept an open mind, and eventually found extraordinary chenille from Spain with a tight, fine hand. It looked like linen but it was cool to the touch and had a soft luster. I decided to use it for a slipcover so it could be washed and have a just-thrown-on feel, like a chic wrap tossed around your shoulders.

Once the walls, sofa, and ottoman were taken care of, I needed some more color. I do love gray but decided to "cheat it" for the window drapes and club chairs using a slightly more light-hearted sea foamy gray green. If the room were pure gray, yellow, and white, it might read a little glum, like old newsprint. I found a reversible fabric with a natural backside, meaning the curtains could be hemmed to create a contrasting border. It blended perfectly with the driftwood finish of a pair of lamps and bird decoys. A real bamboo pole and rings were used for the curtain hardware; woven-grass shades completed the slightly playful jungle vibe.

The room needed some unexpected drama, some *spine.* I chose a totally different color, deep purple brown, to lacquer side tables that sit on either side of the sofa. To reference the color around the room, I found a woven cotton tiger print in the same raisin color. The texture mimics needlepoint, so while it is traditional in construction, it's funky in a glam "look at me" way. Still, as tiger prints go, it is more "Will you have a cocktail?" and less "Jump in the Rover and join me on safari." Perfect for a matched pair of modern French salon-style armchairs.

I covered two very high wing-backed chairs in a gold-brown shiny silk velvet—an almost antique-looking fabric just as glamorous as it is library cozy. There is nothing more sensuous, sinuous, or fluid than silk velvet. This fabric catches light in a very special way and over time takes on an aristocratic, worn look. Here, the material highlights the spectacular architecture of the Seth Stevens'–designed Mr. and Mrs. Chairs.

I went back to a steely gray for the substantial (40-by-60-inch) coffee table. It is wrapped in linen and then lacquered so it's rich and slightly glossy, but the casual burlaplike linen texture is still visible. Because people will sit on this table and put their feet on it, it can't be delicate— it's got to be sturdy and friendly.

Finally, I snuck some cranberry, terra-cotta, and black into the room via accessories. A slightly absurd trim on the throw pillow looked as if it came from another room, another scheme, another shopping trip, and had only landed on the sofa because the mistress of the house loved it and didn't care that it was not part of the scheme.

The journey we embark on in this book will make the process I've just described seem perfectly sensible and intuitive. The path begins when you open your eyes.

When in Doubt, Go Small

People rarely err in buying furniture that is too small. Mistakes happen when they overestimate what will fit into their rooms. Allow yourself a few extra inches of space when buying major pieces (sofas, chairs, coffee tables). Remember, as in cooking, it is easier to add than to take away. Later, you can fill in blank spaces with accessories—a tiny plant stand, a magazine rack—if necessary.

OPPOSITE, CLOCKWISE FROM ABOVE LEFT *Bands of ornate but matte finished trim, vertically set, add detail to a simple linen pillow; a slipcover is beach-house practical but still finely tailored and doesn't feel sloppy; wrapped in lacquered linen, this Asian style coffee table is a versatile and extremely durable staple.*

Ideas: Inspiration and Influences

Chapter Three

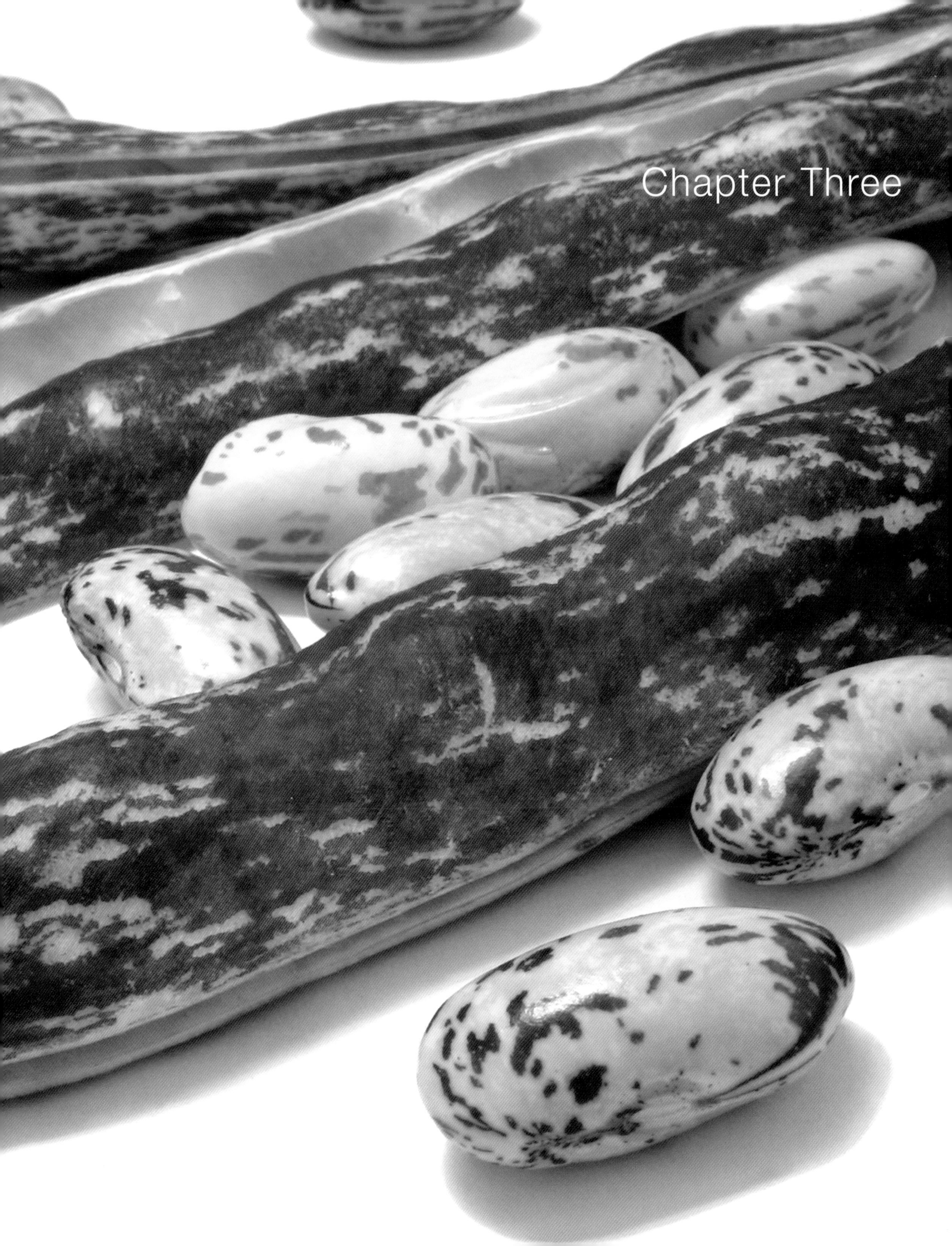

Conventional wisdom about the search for identity says that to find your creative spark you must look within yourself. I find the opposite to be true. The most confident and innovative personal style comes from people who stretch their vision, extend their field of influence, borrow liberally, and revisit preconceived notions and opinions. Open yourself to inspiration!

Like an amuse-bouche before dinner, meant to tease the taste buds and induce mouthwatering hankerings, external inspiration stimulates the senses into a state of hyperawareness. Many of my clients awake to the first stages of aesthetic consciousness when they begin the design processes in their own homes and start to look at the details that surround them with new understanding, appreciation, and purpose.

When I was a child, my mother taught me to see the world with an artist's eye—to collect color and impressions as if my memory were a camera, recording details of the extraordinary houses she showed me. The development of a personal visual library as you travel, study, and experience life is the most powerful resource of individual style. Now, I deliberately, methodically snap photos or draw quick sketches when I'm struck or particularly inspired by something.

Even the smallest objects can provide a backstory for a design philosophy. In my case, for example, there's the heirloom wax bean—the contrasts and colors of this delicate bean, the vivid and subtle veining patterns moving across the surface. . . . There is something slightly errant, chaotic about its appearance, but also a seamless mesh of functionality and beauty. What seems initially unimportant or ordinary can be transformative—with close focus, you gain appreciation of the object's visual attributes. Hearty and sustaining as food, the bean is naturally adorned with markings that have a delicacy and modernity that suits me, and that's how I came to the pattern that is the cover of this book.

The pantry isn't the only place to dig around for your design persona. Small boutiques and even Web pages can introduce big-city ideas to rural outposts. The Internet gives us access to tiny far-off stores, out-of-print design books, and back issues of magazines. Bloggers, designers, and other opinion makers share tips, images, and sources. The early trends, new materials, and cutting-edge designs can be found everywhere on the Web.

OPPOSITE
These samples from my Schumacher and Valtekz fabric lines prove inspiration can be found anywhere. The London tube–inspired maze merges with the graphic citrine trellis pattern; a vintage architectural grate inspired the embroidered serpentine blue swirls; the idea for the ostrich leg pattern came straight from the bird itself; clouded Ikat-like dots resemble dandelion heads; and a glimmer of platinum and bronze overlays semiprecious jewel tones in linens.

Out of Reach but Not Out of Mind

Seeing, wanting, lusting for furniture, art, and design elements is part of the learning process. Much great design is found at unobtainable prices or hidden in private collections. I don't view either as an insurmountable problem. Instead, I try to make the most of every encounter with an object I like, whether or not I can have it, buy it for a client, or find it again. It is important to always be receptive to new visual impressions. Rare and beautiful objects like the one-of-a-kind $48,000 French dresser I saw at an antiques show feed my imagination and give me a new point of reference for quality, color, design, and detail. They simmer in my imagination until I can find the right occasion and materials to re-create the feeling they inspired, either for a client or for a new piece of furniture in my line. (If you can't go to the shows, you can usually view the auction previews online or in catalogs.)

ABOVE
*The worn saffron, olive, and
aubergine colors in this
antique rug gave instant
warmth and gravitas to an
entire den.*

OPPOSITE
*A primitive and weathered
milking stool lends humility
to a newly constructed
kitchen. It almost makes you
feel that the milk in this
room will taste sweeter
than most.*

Shop Talk

Fortunately, big retailers and their happy-medium-meets-middle-of-the-road designs are not the only option for people who live outside the epicenters of design. Nowadays, the shopping experience is exceptionally diverse both in method and range of goods available. Even if you don't have the myriad visionary stores that New York City does, you can have their sensibility mailed to you in catalogs or tap into them online.

There's No Place Like Home

Don't forget to check out the trend-setters in your town; boutiques and antiques shops that catch your eye are worth exploring in detail. Their owners are like art gallery curators who get caught up in creating interesting environments and infusing them with the aesthetic their goods represent.

It is not just the products that get creative juices flowing; sometimes the ever-changing design of the store itself can offer inspiration. Hotel lobbies; restaurants; store-window displays; or furniture retailers like Z Gallerie, Anthropologie, Crate & Barrel, Pier 1, Pottery Barn, Restoration Hardware, Target, JC Penney, Macy's, or Bloomingdales; or your local design boutiques, have cutting-edge stylists or designers who are often given great creative berth to create imaginary interiors within store displays.

The benefit of looking at "public design" is that it's like a free pass into a designer's studio or a tour of a show house. It doesn't matter where you fall on the income spectrum, there is always something to be gained from looking at every level of retail—from high-end boutiques, auction houses, and catalogs, to home-furnishing chain stores and dusty, jumbled vintage shops.

It is unfair, even pretentious, for me as a designer to declare definitively what is acceptable and what is not. But, I think it is uninspired and visually boring to decorate exclusively by label, brand, or provenance. This impulse can be hard to resist, because advertising makes it easy to identify with a style or brand. Consumerism has become central to self-image and how we communicate with one another: people sometimes confuse owning the same pair of shoes or carrying the same designer bag with sharing the same values.

At the same time, there has been a recent shift in age-old views of status. The distinction between highbrow and lowbrow has been eradicated by a new cultural landscape, for better and for worse. High-end designers are showing lines at big discount retailers, making luxury brand names available to all economic brackets. Everyone wants taste, and sometimes this gets translated into everyone having a version, either custom or mass-produced, of the same thing. It takes courage and confidence in your individuality to break away and create unique, personal rooms, to mix branded elements with more unrecognizable or one-of-a-kind elements.

I warn people to open their mail-order catalogs knowing that in two years' time, much of what is shown will be ubiquitous. In an overscheduled world, ordering the backdrop of your life from a catalog is appealing, but there is a lead-weight quality to a home furnished entirely from two or three sources.

Of course, when I open my catalogs each month, I don't lament the bland menu. I admit to twinges of envy for the orderliness, coordination, and calm of a catalog's domestic landscapes.

I admire those rooms, with their computer-graphic balanced scales, their domestic panoramas so flawlessly lit that not a shadow confuses the focus. No clutter or extraneous toys hint at the tangle of true-life compromises or responsibilities that complicate a real functioning household even as they enliven it. Yes, but . . . I remind myself that the photos are not of homes but of carefully constructed sets. It *looks* as if every need is met, but there are only two walls (which are fake), and never any windows or doors in odd places to contend with.

On the glossy pages of a new catalog, the familiar small, framed black-and-white photograph hanging above the beige sofa never looks boring and cold. The text on the page balances the generic image and makes it seem more substantial. The accessories have a haphazard warmth and look as though they were picked up on a trip around the world. Don't fall for it. Once you toss the packing materials and the items take up residence in your house, the "vintage-style" alarm clock and overscale magnifying glass that seemed like wry accents on the side table on page 18 of the catalog instead give off the sad aura of being manufactured by the thousands in a factory. Shake your head and remind yourself that you are reading *the photo and page layout*, not the room. It is at once perfect and empty, the stylistic version of fast food. Most of us are past believing there is any nutrition in it, but the illusion of being complete, comfortable, and familiar can be overpowering, like the aroma of McDonald's French fries when you're starving.

Another unexpected pitfall of filling a room with catalog items is that almost everything has the same expiration date. Like a closet full of baby-doll dresses, cap sleeves, and suits with wide lapels, the trend goes stale one day, and nothing you have is wearable. Mass-market furniture does not hold its value either, and you will notice the moment your feelings change as glaringly as you would if all the lightbulbs in your house were to falter at once. Your friends (and everyone else's) are ordering the same thing or seeing it advertised so frequently that eventually the entire nation feels as if they've visited that lifeless, storyless room a million times.

Newness is the catalog inventory's greatest asset. In fifteen months, when the mass-produced item has lost its only luster, you'll be tired of it. Finding one-of-a-kind items may cost you more in time, if not dollars, than shopping off the shelf, but divide the up-front costs by the extra years of longevity and you will discover the price per year of use is far lower. The 1960s-style reproduction brown wooden kitchen chair or the faux vintage metal garden gate "wall art" from a catalog ends up costing more because you grow weary of it in short order and then buy something else to replace it. A splurge from a boutique, flea market, or auction tells the story of your discovery. Over the years it may move with you from room to room, house to house, or even in and out of storage, picking up history and taking a place of honor in your life.

Manufacturers are responding to the increasing mainstream interest in and knowledge about design. As a result, the styling of mass-market furniture these days can be remarkable. For this reason, a basic element like a chair or sofa, bought to fill an immediate need or to act as a placeholder until something really perfect comes along, is great. But if you are hoping to make your purchases last a decade, avoid the instant gratification of catalogs, hold out for love, and hit garage sales, thrift stores, flea markets, Craigslist, or eBay for your cheap and quick fixes.

Sometimes things are bought or held not because they are "right" but because they are loved. The room with a wobbly chair and a mismatched but delightfully shaped sofa is both comfort-

OPPOSITE, ABOVE
Brilliant mid-century light fixture reproductions, gilt bamboo molding, cream lacquer walls, and tall leaning mirrors define the elegant, soothing, and very feminine De Bernedinis Salon in New York City.

OPPOSITE, BELOW
Richter's Jewelry Store in Palm Beach shows how the use of silver leaf, antique mirror, sisal, lacquer, and Lucite can combine to make a very pretty, light-handed glamour.

FOLLOWING PAGES
The mix of 1960s mod, 1980s graphic boldness, and an industrial loft creates a zesty, dramatic, and fun shopping experience in the New York City Alice & Olivia store.

ing and welcoming. As in *The Velveteen Rabbit,* the truest beauty lies in the sentimental value we place on things we cherish. Items with a past help tell an ongoing story, unlike a room full of things that were manufactured last month or bought only for their pedigree and status. Eclectic rooms, developed over time, or created with items that have had previous lives, present a dynamic narrative. Of course, there is a difference between the wear and tear of love and pure dilapidation and carelessness. But old pieces always have more soul. Oscar Wilde said he liked men with a future and women with a past. The best furniture has both.

I've got nothing against new furnishings and use reproductions frequently. Try to buy something that is more than just an obvious knockoff, something that has its own unique style. Independent boutiques sell furniture and accessories with more subtlety and eccentricity than "big box" retailers. They have the freedom to experiment and take more risks because they don't have to preorder 100,000 of an item eighteen months in advance. With faster turnover, the end result is smaller stock but greater variety and more exciting choices. Look online at design blogs such as www.designspongeonline.com, www.thenestmaker.com, www.apartmenttherapy.com, and http://allthebest2007.blogspot.com for their highlighted product links to specialized shops that ship nationally. The color in a contemporary artist's glass vase or the print in a new line of fabric may lead your room in an exciting fresh direction.

Items from boutiques, flea markets, vintage and antiques stores, and auctions, and roadside finds also help you connect with historical styles, past lives, and more offbeat aesthetics. I shop in these places by eye, not by provenance. In New York City, I love learning from my favorite antiques dealers; at 145 Antiques, Coconut & Co., Lars Bolander, Mondo Cane, Duane, Mantiques Modern, Amy Perlin, and Sentimento. They have helped me appreciate different kinds of furniture, the quality and history of antiques, and how to creatively juxtapose them. Seasonal vintage jaunts include Dixie Highway in West Palm Beach; LaBrea in Los Angeles, as well as Chapman Radcliff, Dragonette, Downtown, and Blackman Cruz, where I always stop in when I'm in town; upstate New York back roads; and European flea markets.

I feel a great victory when I have found a one-off item or resurrected something old and forgotten in a junk store and rediscovered its beauty. Your own weird, quirky junk found at flea markets or during an after-work Dumpster-diving expedition is more likely to appreciate in value (and not just monetary value) than the taupe sectional everyone is ordering. Enthusiasm for something that becomes a commodity, or that could be seen as home "merchandise," is unlikely to grow and usually only diminishes. The feeling you have for something more unique will expand and deepen as the years go by.

About five years ago I found a gourd-shaped lamp made of parchment at Mantiques Modern in New York. It was gaggingly unaffordable. The mottled caramel color with gentle crazing under layers of clear varnish and its stocky but graceful profile spoke poetry to me. To others it may have appeared no different from countless other cream-colored table lamps, but for some reason I knew when I saw it that it was *mine.* I knew if I didn't act, it would fester in an uncomfortable "gone but not forgotten" section of my memory. Naturally, I bought it. When I come home at night and sink into our sofa, my eye is always drawn to it on the side table next to me—something solid that resonates with a beauty that maybe only I perceive. As you may

Celerie Stalks at Midnight

I do more and more shopping on Internet auction sites and online "garage sales" and cyber space–only retailers. Best feature: it can be done anytime the mood strikes or there's a quiet moment—in my house, that's usually in the wee hours. My favorites:

www.cbellfurnishing.com   www.1stdibs.com   www.145antiques.com
www.christies.com   www.lahardware.com   www.sentimentoantiques.com
www.demolitiondepot.com   www.mantiquesmodern.com   www.sothebys.com
www.doylenewyork.com   www.mondocane.com
www.ebay.com   www.oldegoodthings.com

imagine, I've had my head turned by more than a few other lamps since I found that one, but it has become one of the elements that makes home, home and me, me. This is the kind of object love you must indulge—though you can't know where it will lead, follow the voice of the lamp (or rug, or chest of drawers, or amateur painting) that sings clearly to you.

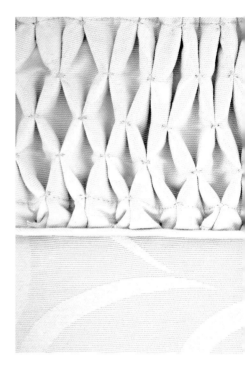

Attending auctions and flipping through the catalogs of auction houses have proven great sources of inspiration and ideas, whether I've ultimately bought from them or not. Look for local estate-sale auctions. In New York City, just about every other Friday, Tepper Galleries previews the goods to be sold the next day. It's a killer estate-sale auction experience, where you can buy furniture and accessories that go home with you immediately without paying painful prices and feeling like a big-city fool.

Many New York antiques dealers do their own shopping at that sale and other "arcade" or house auctions. Loyal attendance at them can mean a splendid apartment without a fat bank account. The quality and look of items vary wildly, as they do in most auctions, but that's part of the fun. Bidding requires you to be rational and impulsive at the same time, because victorious absentee bids can surprise you on Monday. Auctions at Doyle, Wright, Rago, Sotheby's, and Christie's are entertainment in and of themselves, and offer a surprising variety of items at every price point—you would be amazed at the high quality and unusual furniture and accessories you can afford.

Then of course, there are salvagers, who save and resell parts of old houses and commercial spaces before they are demolished. These are great sources for vintage hardware, plumbing parts and supplies, fireplace mantels, doors, hinges, knobs, lighting, paneling, moldings, and anything else you can think of that is part of the structure, architecture, and design of building.

Because I am a professional shopper, I have given myself permission to buy things on a whim if they move me. I sometimes feel like a social worker for furniture and objects, finding happy homes for those I've fallen in love with unexpectedly. At other times, I feel more like an omnivorous, insatiable woman with huge storage bills and lots of junk, but it's working so far because I've managed to find a caregiver for every piece I've adopted. Sometimes, I see something that is so off (without crossing the line into total kitsch) that I have to buy it—such as an old farm sign or an amateur landscape or a floral oil painting. Or Cupid's arrow strikes my funny bone instead of my heart—they're both equally persuasive. To handle overflow, I have instituted a foster-care policy with the girls from my office, who go home with had-to-have-it-couldn't-pass-it-up items until I find the right home for them.

Keeping Old Customs Alive

Mass manufacturing and economies of scale have made good design available at every level. There are signs that the democratization of good designs offered through DWR, Pottery Barn, Martha Stewart, Target, IKEA, etc., has improved taste around the world. But the huge volume and scale of production has caused a loss of craftsmanship. Big-factory assembly lines are built to move things along quickly: paint has to dry as fast as possible, joints need to be nailed together pneumatically, screw holes must be automatically filled and sealed at lightning speed. Such urgency often means a sacrifice of longevity and durability. Foam cushions decompose, cracks appear after a year or two, joints loosen, and the most saleable aesthetics push out the more unique or idiosyncratic elements of distinguished design.

Custom work, on the other hand, means handwork. Extra time is required for artisans to practice their craft, which naturally means greater expense, but the resulting pieces are more durable, distinctive, and specific to your needs. A built-in bookcase integrates beautifully into a room's existing architecture while making the most of available space, whereas a bookcase taken home in a flat-pack box and assembled on site will always look comparatively flimsy, delineated by the shadow cast on the wall behind it. It will never have the stature of a cabinet that is part of the room. Custom work also gives you more quality control—when something goes wrong, you know who is responsible and who can fix it.

An unusual space or exacting standards may necessitate custom millwork, upholstery, or hardware, but most high-end custom-goods suppliers in major cities work only through designers. I am often asked why "to the trade" is not "open to all." Most of the reasons are cost related. Getting connected to the retail market requires sales, marketing, and advertising budgets that would drive the already-precious price higher, and retail customers require hand-holding that would pull highly skilled workers from their craft. Helping clients develop the vocabulary of personal preferences is one of my favorite responsibilities, and I have heard from many custom workrooms that they prefer to work with designers who understand the value and variety of the workroom's output without a sales pitch.

Made-to-order furniture and bespoke upholstery cost more than assembly-line goods for a reason. When a client asks me with incredulity why his pair of 22-inch throw pillows costs more than $700, I am not unsympathetic. Let's follow a custom-made pillow through its journey and you may decide that the price is a bargain, considering how far the item has traveled from inception to your sofa and how long lasting and beautiful the end product will be.

First, the fabric is designed and woven in very small quantities (usually only a few hundred yards at a time), costing approximately $100 a yard. The beautiful textile is generally constructed out of a natural fiber such as silk, mohair, wool, or cotton. The price per yard reflects the commodity price of the construction materials as well as the research, artwork, machinery costs, factory overhead, and labor to create that fabric; plus the shipping from Italy, France, Spain, or any number of other places around the world, sometimes with significant import taxes; exchange rates; the overhead of all the businesses involved (staff! health insurance! rent! advertising!); and then some profit to make it all worthwhile. (The fabric and trim

OPPOSITE AND ABOVE
The smallest details of ornament, like smocking on a curtain valance or the trim on a pillow, add the dominant personality particular to each room. For instance, the dark bobble trim on this floral pillow makes it appropriate for a woody, leathery den.

FOLLOWING PAGE
There is precision and artistry (even surgery) involved in quality construction.

ABOVE

In what feels like a dating-show lineup of upholstery options, four different personalities of club chairs are apparent when they're stripped down to their muslin "birthday suits" and stand side by side. I like to present my clients with a sit test of at least ten different chairs in the custom workroom, because sometimes a bottom can be as discriminating as an eye. And it is then possible to tailor the scale, pitch, arm and leg style, back height, seat width and depth, and fill of each of these chairs to suit the height, taste, and purpose of each client and each room.

that go into two pillows cost about $500.00.) Four sides of two 22-inch pillows require about 1½ yards of fabric at $100.00 per yard plus five yards of $35.00-per-yard trim. Add to that the cost of the down pillow form and labor-intensive hand cutting and finishing.

You or your designer must then spend the time to search through the multitude of options, select a favorite that fits a very restricted set of aesthetic demands, place the order for both the fabric and the trim, and supervise its delivery to a seamstress or a fabricator. The maker will then cut the fabric and trims to the designer's specifications and create the form, which may require special sewing techniques such as pleats, or a unique shape, such as a box or a ball. Since the pillow is custom designed, the soft but tight cotton lining (called down proofing) and fill must also be specially made. If it is, as I prefer to use, a 100 percent down pillow (from a goose that was fed, cared for, *and* plucked on a farm somewhere), the price is higher because it does not have the cheap bulk of extraneous quill.

Each component of the pillow must go from farm to mill to artist to store to designer to fabricator, through multiple shippers, layers of invoicing, and the labor of tracking and coordinating in order to arrive at your house. Can you believe all of that time and work goes into a pillow? And that it *only costs about $350?*

To the Trade

One of my most prized sources of inspiration is the sometimes hidden workrooms and studios where artisans craft everything from custom upholstery to lighting fixtures to wallpaper using age-old methods and secret formulas. These "to the trade only" establishments work *exclusively* with design professionals and architects. The level of quality and workmanship they provide is unsurpassed and generally unavailable at the retail or consumer level.

Custom objects are admittedly luxuries—yet they can last more than a lifetime and become part of the permanent features of a home,

passed down from generation to generation. A well-made pillow, a finely wrought brass doorknob (that has not been lacquered over to unnaturally preserve its finish forever), a hand-sewn lampshade, or hand-printed wallpaper never *really* goes out of fashion.

For a peek into the slightly mysterious and romantic world of "to the trade only" artisans, turn the page and come with me to the late-nineteenth-and early-twentieth-century brick-and-stone buildings in the heart of Manhattan that house the craftspeople, both young and old, who practice skills that can only be learned by apprenticing with masters.

Fashion Trend

New York's fashion world is an active and unpredictable muse. In my designs, I strive to translate my love for it with a chic but warm aesthetic. I have deep admiration for fashion designers and keep an eye on the shifting trends like any indulgent fashionista, except that I am always looking for inspiration from the silhouettes, colors, cut, and details. Show me a fabulous new skirt and I think of lampshades. A jeweled neckline, and I'm off on trimmings or nail heads.

These days, trends in runway fashion and the home-furnishings business inform each other. This dialogue happens immediately, without an intervening season for the influence to be felt, translated, and applied. We all know what everyone else is doing because trends that appear in studios or on runways are reported in real time, instantly across the world.

Certain pattern and color trends, attitude shifts, and renewed interest in specific time periods (English Regency, 1950s American) emerge on the runway and in the showroom. Over the last couple of years, we have begun to see more conversation between the worlds of style and home design. Window-and-door hardware inspires details on fashion accessories such as grommets and chains on handbags, jeans, belts, and shoes. In interior design editorial spreads, you can see the season's glimmering nail polish and eye makeup colors popping up in throw pillows and rugs. The color stories, fabric sheens, and use of metallics, menswear staples, and patent leathers are increasingly similar across both worlds.

Appreciation for fashion design is one reason why textiles play such an important part in all of my design schemes. You can tap the vein of inspiration by taking an electronic stroll around www.style.com or the latest fashion magazines. A classic YSL suit might inspire a lux but tailored bedroom with classic lines and crisp trim. A Catherine Malandrino dress represents a perfect color palette for a dining room—all silvery gray and purple. Dressmaker details on a Lela Rose blouse can be interpreted as tucks and pleats on upholstery pieces.

Substance Over Style

I don't care about "in" and "out" as concepts. If a piece of furniture or an accessory is authentic, gorgeous, expressive, or fun, don't worry about whether it is on trend or off. By the time you get it settled, the list will have changed anyway!

Reading the Current Scene

I travel constantly, and my journeys bring me a flood of new ideas and inspiration. Even the hours trapped in an airplane are productive, though I would hate to be the person sitting next to me as I rip from magazines page after page of striking images that serve as reminders, ideas, and inspiration. Consulting an array of stylistically different design books and magazines will help you come up with your personal design Rorschach test.

Magazines like *Domino, Dwell, House Beautiful, Metropolitan Home, Elle Decor, World of Interiors, Traditional Home, O at Home, Veranda, Southern Accents,* and *In Style Home* spotlight the contemporary vernacular and help you determine your own taste. If you gravitate toward the disciplined modern mastery of *Metropolitan Home,* you are likely a controlled minimalist. Or if you love the mix-and-match sensibility of *Domino,* you may be more willing to buck the system, flirt with fashion, and come up with your own tweaked style.

Get a sense of what you respond to in the marketplace by tearing out the pictures of rooms and objects you like from these publications. Then view the cuttings and watch for a theme or pattern to emerge. That exploration can begin your vision for a room or an entire house or serve as the impetus for an intense dialogue between a husband and wife with different tastes. Generally you will gain a better understanding of how flamboyant, organic, fashionable, "contemporary," modern, or traditional you skew. Keep a folder or a drawer to store this visual diary of your changing tastes.

How adventurous are you willing to be? If you repeatedly wrinkle your nose at mid-century pictures (viewing them as uncomfortable or too retro), then don't get trapped into the look by one-off impulse. An Eames chair or a Saarinen table may grab you in a particular setting—the design equivalent of a one-night stand—but if it is inconsistent with your overall aesthetic, you may be frustrated down the road with such an iconic element of a style you don't adore.

If you find yourself plucking pages with a consistent style or find it mixed artfully with others you like, consider this a green light to use it as part of your vocabulary. If you love the feel of "shabby chic" but prefer tailored lines, look for successful executions of rooms lavished with soft textures and feminine florals that haven't succumbed to the overstuffed tendencies of enormous upholstery swathed in baggy slipcovers.

Nondesign periodicals can provide insights as well. In magazine ads and editorial profiles from the 1980s, people were often shown getting out of a car or a plane or sitting on the deck of a yacht. There was nothing particularly personal about these images; they were all about conveying power and status. Now magazines like *Vanity Fair, Town and Country, W, Vogue, Harpers Bazaar, Lucky,* even *People* often show their subjects at home, as a way of illuminating their character through their personal space. In our overly busy, distracted society, people feel immense nostalgia for a private life. Today's celebrity magazines know that fans are sometimes as interested in fantasizing about the rich and imaginative domestic lives of stars as they are their trysts. As a result, the newsstand offers you a look at the most current design work. What was once off-limits or considered deeply private gets offered up for your design edification by style mavens, power brokers, home owners, editors, and lifestyle-oriented advertising.

Newly published design books also let you travel the world and gain access to rooms and pore over details that would otherwise be impossible to see. Recent books I recommend are by Rose Tarlow, Kelly Wearstler, Vicente Wolfe, Jeffrey Bilhuber, Charlotte Moss, Colefax and Fowler, Marietta Himes Gomez, Bunny Williams, and Jonathan Adler.

I also often find myself drifting back in time for research, ideas, and reference points. As with items in a flea market, out-of-print books and vintage magazines provide now-forgotten combinations and looks that sometimes seem modern or fresh today. Trends that seem new have almost always had previous lives. Dorothy Draper's *Decorating Is Fun!,* Elsie de Wolfe's *The*

Inspiration is just a way to jog your memory, and to open your eyes to what is not directly in front of you. It is using the narrative of your life as a palette from which to choose ideas.

ABOVE

I worked with a client by tearing out images from design magazines to come up with a room that mixes Chinese Chippendale and Hollywood Regency. For example, the design for the bookcases was found in one such tear sheet, translated and enlarged to fit the niches on either side of the fireplace.

House in Good Taste, Russel Wright's *Good Design Is for Everyone,* Edith Wharton's *The Decoration of Houses* (written in 1897), *Francis Elkins: Interior Design,* and so many others provide insight and ideas that may seem as fresh now as they were when originally published.

For the past six months I have kept a 1960s *Better Homes & Gardens* decorating guide on my desk. Looking at images of old rooms exercises the eye and allows you to revisit preconceived notions about design and taste. I used to think 1950s and '60s Danish modern furniture looked rigid, cold, lofty, and not homey at all; recent catalogs and magazines have been featuring it in harshly minimalist settings. But as I looked through the decorating guide, seeing this kind of furniture in the context of its era reminded me of its potential for warmth.

LEFT AND OPPOSITE
A trip to Portofino inspired palette and design details on a poolside Palm Beach loggia (opposite). A digital camera records delightful elements to be incorporated in the space (this page, clockwise from top left): a sunburned color palette, a scalloped Juliet balcony, inlaid stone patterns, and a triumphant trompe l'oeil painted facade on a simple shuttered building.

Have Passport, Will Design

My greatest extravagance and pleasure has always been travel. It's in my blood: my maternal great-grandparents spent their life in the hotel business, and my grandfather was known for travel-napping his children and spontaneously jumping on trains to hastily planned destinations often without luggage. As a child, my mother spent the first day of many spontaneous trips shopping with her mother for underwear and a toothbrush.

Perhaps because my family had strong roots at home, we did not feel the need to return to any one place repeatedly. Instead, my parents turned every trip into a different adventure and opportunity for new sensations. Whether our excursions were domestic jaunts to visit friends in the Adirondacks, Idaho, Maine, or Newport or on Nantucket or Martha's Vineyard or far-flung voyages to the Dordogne, Germany, Hong Kong, Italy, New Zealand, or Argentina, each year brought something different. We found ways to delve into the glamour of far-off places without breaking the bank. People often think of certain spots as off-limits because of their expense, but when I was a kid, my parents would find ways to make our budget travels rich in impressions but affordable. We would drop by Maxim's for dessert after eating dinner at a neighborhood bistro, or visit storied, architecturally significant hotels such as Georges V for tea during the day, while staying at a pensione for the night.

The objective was to see and experience the most amazing places, even if only for a glimpse or a taste. I try to keep on that path. Once a year I take a special "girls only" trip with my mother and my sister; the rule is that the destination must be somewhere we have never been before. Our most recent excursion was to Marrakech. The colors, textures, and patterns have already found their way into some of my room designs.

Certain spots demand repeated visits. In Paris I cannot go a block without taking pictures of storefronts or of displays in antiques shops, and I keep a filing cabinet in my head of what I see. I have no plans to open a store at the moment, but if I ever change my mind, I know just the storefront I would want. A photo of it awaits in one of my many souvenir boxes. So snap or sketch away—the images don't have to be perfect, just good enough to jog your memory when you're back home and trying to recall the rug in the hotel lobby, or the ironwork on a side street. Digital cameras, pocket-small but of seemingly infinite memory, are quickly becoming an electronic replacement for the scratch pad and sketchbook.

I am lucky to have a visual memory, and I remember every house I've ever visited. Chances are you, too, have strong recollections of rooms or houses you've admired. What you weave into your own home design is more meaningful if it is in tribute to your memories.

Google It

Browsing through a used bookstore is a joy; unexpected discoveries are always exciting. But sometimes you want to locate a specific title or concept, and the Internet has made finding out-of-print design volumes easier and more systematic. Rare-book dealers have gone online, making it easier to find what you are looking for and compare prices. Blogs, published research, and fan sites provide a lot of information about past design and designers. I also peruse designers' Web sites in search of looks I love. Here's my guide to just a few of the best style makers of the twentieth century—yesterday, today, and tomorrow:

Thomas O'Brien—Contemporary classic with a broad but tasteful product line.

Colefax and Fowler—Classic English style characterized by deep, comfy upholstery; saturated color; bold prints; and strong, traditional furniture lines.

Sister Parrish—English country house style made classically American. Jacqueline Kennedy's decorator.

Albert Hadley—The late Sister Parrish's design partner, with wide-ranging talents and an enduring voice in the field.

Polly Jessup—A Palm Beach designer who uses English antiques mixed with custom-made pieces, expensive fabrics, matching floral chintzes for draperies, and overstuffed chairs, floral rugs, and botanical prints. Most famous for adding dressmaking details to upholstery.

David Hicks—Colorful, classic, geometric style; symmetrical.

Rachel Ashwell—English-born California girl who blended UK tradition with LA ease and came up with Shabby Chic; white-painted furniture, pastels, slipcovers, flowers, and simplicity.

Kelly Wearstler—Modern design glamorized with theatrical color and scale.

Elsie de Wolfe—Early 1900s American designer who advocated soft colors for walls, bright chintzes for curtains and furniture, Colonial and European (particularly French) antiques and painted furniture, porcelain bowls, and flowers.

Dorothy Draper—Mid-twentieth-century designer who loved bright colors, theatrically scaled white-painted wood furniture, and floral prints.

Steven Gambrel—Playfully mixes vintage, antique, and modern pieces and vibrant color to create comfortable rooms in urban and country settings.

Jeffrey Bilhuber—Warm American modern mixed with earthy elements.

Bunny Williams—Comfortable, classic; known for her traditional American country house look.

Charlotte Moss—More great American design tradition—floral, feminine, but never fussy.

Rose Tarlow—Modern rooms with rich texture and warm tones.

Harry Bertoia—Sculpture and furniture designer whose medium was metal, including one of the most comfortable chairs known to man, which he designed in the 1950s and is still being produced today, to spiritual sculptures made in the 1970s.

Grossfield House—1960s–1970s furniture company that made theatrical styles. Lucite knobs, inlaid leather, lacquer.

Ruthie Sommers—As varied and eclectic as she is classic. "Pretty and decisively feminine."

William "Billy" Haines—Former actor turned Hollywood decorator; his luxe, glam rooms are the inspiration for today's "modern glamour" Hollywood Regency look.

Tony Duquette—"Magical" is not an exaggerated description of the interiors, handmade jewelry, and furniture that this master of glamour and modernity created. Truly a design genius.

The pale blue living room of a childhood friend may have delighted you for years. Allow that response to steer your selection of paint chips to sample on your new walls. Or, send a Pantone book to your friend's mother and ask her to find the closest match. Ransack your memory for design elements that excite you. Describing the winding staircase at an uncle's Victorian heap, long since fallen under the wrecking ball, can be more useful to an architect designing your house than any catalog of balustrades—and the more specific you are in your descriptions, the more likely you are to get the staircase of your dreams.

The houses in our memory are not the only ones that can affect our design choices. Draw inspiration from existing homes. Old houses tend to have character-filled auras. Show houses, architectural societies, preservation houses, garden club tours, and even charity house tours (for example, both Manhattan and Brooklyn have summer brownstone tours of private residences, as do other cities) allow access to any number of design ideas and perspectives. Even the most humble design detail, like a glass doorknob or wainscoting spied while touring a Newport summer "cottage" (read: mansion), can project strong personality because of the imprint that the house's owners have left.

A visit to a residence you have never seen before can completely alter and stretch preconceived notions. My husband and I were invited to a very modern house in Texas for a friend's anniversary party not long ago. The hosts had transformed an old pump house on their property—kind of like a bunker open to the sky—into a party space. Tall rebar and concrete beams protruded from normally empty pools that they had filled with 6 inches of water. At night, the pools caught the reflection of video artist Jennifer Steinkamp's projection on the wall of a tree swaying in the breeze.

I had never felt moved by any video art I had seen in art museums and galleries, and I usually shy away from the most brutal modern architecture, but this was instantly mesmerizing. The effect of the ghostly swaying and ebbing of the reflections was both visceral and atmospheric. When I stood in the water surrounded by dancing couples, their movement causing ripples of reflected glimmers across the concrete walls, elements of design I had dismissed and the art form I least appreciated came magically together.

I was seven months' pregnant at the time, so the jalapeño margaritas that were being served to others weren't to blame for my being mesmerized; I was awed by the integration of modern art set into urban modern industrial architecture. Everything I thought I hated became beautiful. I am probably not going to start doing rooms with open ceilings and exposed rebar piercing concrete walls, but I see better how those textures and colors could be used to create evocative results I had never considered possible.

Inspiration is just a way to jog your memory, and to open your eyes to what is not directly in front of you. It is using the narrative of your life as a palette from which to choose ideas. In the creation of your own space, personal meaning is crucial—pulling together odds and ends that you've stumbled across or searched out in zeal. (In my house that means metal flowers, antique shagreen-covered objects, vintage children's games, and scientific relics.) Mixing these with inherited items and brand-new acquisitions adds intimacy, sentimentality, and identity to a room.

This photo illustrates an epiphany for me—a situation in which two elements, previously despised (deconstructed industrial design and video art), merged in one of the most beautiful and magical visions to make me think differently forever about both.

Personal Taste Meets "Good" Taste

Chapter Four

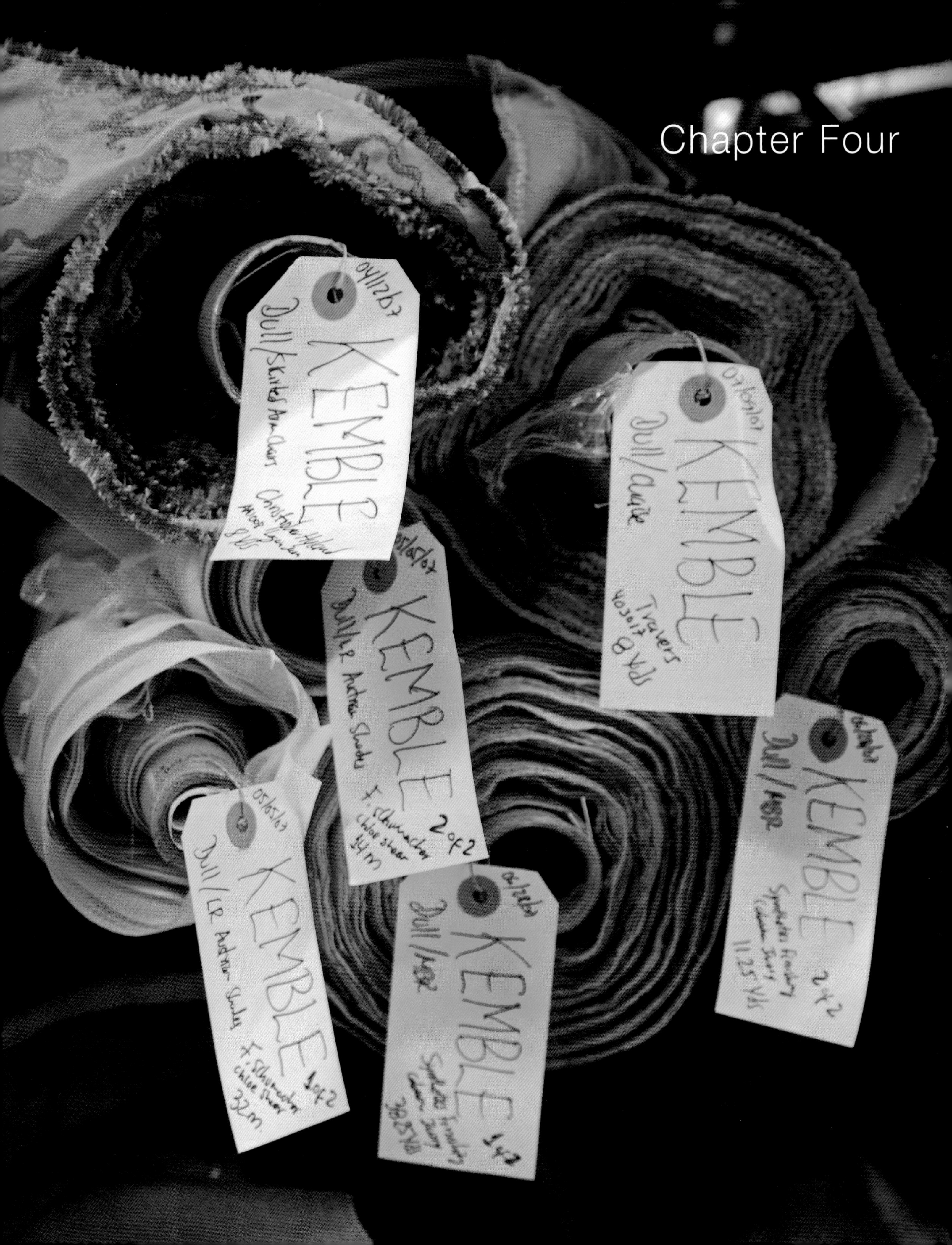

Two different rooms in two different houses—a birch-covered guest bedroom in the Adirondacks (opposite) and a bachelor's Soho loft (above)—show how decorative elements express the vastly differing personalities and purposes of their owners and locations. On the left, the front of a double-sided clock inhabits the living room and its back dominates a sitting area.

One key to exceptional personal style is highlighting individual assets and charms; the same is true when designing a room. While the most interesting rooms express the owner's interests and personality, they also follow a few aesthetic conventions of palette, proportion, and scale, the principles of good taste.

Taste is a loaded word because it can imply judgment and lofty class distinction, and not necessarily in a good way. But without a quality and style judgment, there is no place to begin the discussion. When I talk about taste in terms of interior design, I am referring to the subtleties and defining features of a space. A successful and, yes, tasteful scheme is defined by an interesting conversation between the functional elements in a room (sofa, chairs, tables), personal touches and general stylistic choices (modern, traditional, bohemian, eclectic), and the physical architecture of the room (moldings, windows, walls). That dialogue is what makes a room memorable, engaging, and distinctive.

The conventions of good conversation translate to room design: people speak to each other in even tones of voice (harmonious color schemes) punctuated carefully (symmetry with intriguing variations or accents) and at a well-regulated pace; leave breathing room between sentences (places to rest the eyes before moving on); and enliven the conversation with occasional bursts of exuberance and exclamations. A successful room maintains a conscious interplay with all of these elements. A good room reveals itself like a well-told story—the focus is steady, with no gratuitous digressions (or in the case of a room, too many disparate elements), and its tone has changed to suit its audience (lowering the lights or opening the blinds; pulling up a chair in front of the fire, pushing a table out of the way to make room for an impromptu dance floor).

You can achieve good taste in a room through a deliberate balance of old and new, serious and silly, picked-up-off-the street and custom made. When designing, even at the highest end, I tend not to buy items that all have the same vibration in terms of value, patina, provenance, or "importance." A room that is fancy across the board, or relies too heavily on the same

vocabulary of formality, luxury, and grandeur starts to feel tiresome, like a millionaire dinner partner who drones on incessantly about the tedium of commercial flying. A mix of high and low or practical and sentimental makes for a more interesting and impact-filled room. When I walk into a "too perfect" house, it seems to have no sense of history or future; the rooms are fixed in time and don't look like they have ever changed or ever will. Some are so overcurated that no sense of the owner remains—as if no one is ever home. Though exceptionally well executed in one way, they lack the power and personality to inspire.

A room discloses the record of our deeper history: color and material selections, our personal sense of comfort or formality, and the memories evoked by personal touches, such as collections or the distinctive accessories, like unusual picture frames and vases. Going back to the idea of room as a conversation, I try to put together the words of my story in a new way to express something distinct. I am gathering and juxtaposing the forms and objects uniquely mine—sofa, rug, lamp, pillow—to make the space more evocative, increasing its atmosphere and resonance.

Successful, tasteful rooms share four basic elements—color, texture, arrangement, and accessory. When carefully managed, they produce both comfort and intrigue. Something thrilling occurs when design rules meet personal style and they like each other.

THIS PAGE AND OPPOSITE
Both of these rooms belong to owners who express their interests through collected objects. Opposite, the room reflects an interest in the natural world—assembled prints, paintings, hats, duck decoys, coral, as well as the colors and materials reflect a casual "old Florida" air. The room on this page is a mix of nautical hardware and references repurposed (a porthole becomes a window from shower to bathroom) alongside custom design elements (ebonized and varnished woodwork) to make a boat-meets-bathhouse aesthetic.

Plan a Palette

Fabric is the best way to establish and reinforce the colors you have selected for a room. As in the show-house example, when working with my clients, I first try to find the one extraordinary print or geometric that contains a majority of the colors they would like to see throughout the room. The fabric itself might be used only on a pillow or two. A painting, a photograph of a rug, a picture of a floral arrangement, or even a fashion spread from a magazine can serve the same purpose if you have not yet found the right fabric.

The hues you have chosen help determine what else you need to make the room complete. Look in the background of your fabric or picture to find coordinating versions of neutrals, creams, whites, beiges, browns, grays. You can use them for the elements that take up a lot of space such as the ceiling color, large upholstery pieces, or floor color and curtains. Then, use the other dominant colors from your fabric (or picture) as accents on the smaller-scale elements, such as chairs, pillows, table skirts, or ceramic or glass objects, or on a piece of lacquered furniture.

I have seen great decorators build an entire professional look around a color palette. They also use proportions of color that are repetitive (e.g., 80 percent of a dominant color—10 percent

BELOW AND OPPOSITE
Even the office of Kemble Interiors New York (left) reflects our love of color. Stacks of fabric samples (below) assist us as we create schemes for each client's rooms. Using leathers, grass cloth, wallpaper, ceramic color chips, carpet, and trim for palette planning (opposite).

The Color Guru Speaks

Anytime I have a serious color concern, I confer with my friend, colleague, and custom color mixing genius Christopher Rollinson. Here, he shares some of his favorite thoughts on color:

Visible light travels in waves. We see colors the same way we hear sounds. Compare the amount of light in a room to the volume of a stereo. Turn up the volume and you hear every element of the music. Turn it down low and you may hear only the instruments that were played the loudest when they were recorded. Now think in light. If you have a lot of light, then every color in the room is seen. Dim the light and only the most vibrant colors come through.

Geographic location can determine quality of light. Water reflects 50 percent more light than land, and absorbs the red and warmer spectrum of sunlight, so in a seaside house your white and cream walls may appear gray. Paint in warmer tones to offset warmer light.

Natural light and artificial light act like recorded and live sound. The same music you would hear from a small home stereo sounds very different when you hear it at a live performance. The natural light through your windows is different from that given off by your table lamp. A color will look very different depending on this light source. Even sunlit walls will appear different depending on whether they get southern or northern exposure.

Color changes with the viewing angle. Even adjacent walls will appear subtly different. Color will also appear more intense in a larger space than a small area, because big spaces provide extra area for light to bounce around. Matte finishes appear (lighter) than those with a gloss of the same color due to the amount of reflected light. Because of this I prefer to use light in matte finishes, and if I look for a dark color for high effect I choose a gloss.

Colors don't just evoke feelings and moods, they drive them. Warmer colors will excite the senses while cooler will calm. Light colors give an airy, open feel while darker colors are cozier. Some say lime makes you crazy and pink makes you docile. That's been claim enough to make the latter a popular choice for prison walls.

each of two accent colors). This makes their work instantly recognizable—the brown, aqua, celadon, and white signature of one designer or the constant white, chocolate, and navy of another may overpower the expression of the client's own personality. If you work with a professional, look at as much of their finished work as you can so that you know the difference between their signature and yours. If they are one and the same, all power to you both, but proceed with caution. It's one thing to share a perfume but another to identify so closely with someone that you turn up at a party wearing the same outfit and hairstyle. It is evident (and sad) when someone's home ventriloquizes their designer's tastes.

Rooms that are naturally less fabric intensive, such as entry halls, dining rooms, kitchens, and bathrooms, can take color cues from other details used in those spaces. Lacquer your walls in a color that's used in your favorite china pattern. Or, for a bathroom, use a hue from the marble, granite, slates, or tile for paint and carry over the deeper or lighter tones for wallpaper and towels.

Then, begin working according to the laws of juxtaposition and proximity: don't place one shiny or dull or bright fabric, color, or object next to another unless it is a collection. Don't match your sofa and coffee table. Go with a strong contrast: if the sofa is a warm woven material, I'd look for a higher sheen, slicker coffee table (lacquer, Lucite, glass, metal) rather than something dry like honed marble, an upholstered ottoman, or a matte finished wood.

Find Your Color Courage

I start every project with color. Fear or uncertainty about color leads many people to overdo neutral—cream walls, beige sofa, muted brown-toned furniture—which is not bad but can certainly be boring. Don't let a fear of being tacky render you tasteless. If a color's intensity were rated on a scale of 1 to 10, too many people would end up with nothing but 1s, 2s, and 3s, from untoasted white bread to cream of wheat—blah.

On the other hand, a room filled with saturated deep red, blue, and green—all 8s, 9s, and 10s—is too pungent, like a straight spoonful of Lawry's seasoning, Vegemite, or bouillon—so condensed a reduction that it burns. Try for a varied but balanced "2 (cream)-6 (deep, but neutral)-10 (bright, intense)" palette (light, deep, saturated), whatever the overall look.

There is no reason to follow stuffy conventions when selecting color, as in "dark colors and plaids for men" and "pastels and flowers for girls." A few years ago, some newlywed clients of mine were chomping at the bit to move into their new apartment. They had been living in a small duplex loft apartment where all the rooms opened into one another, which had created a few points of friction between them over the previous year and a half. Their gripes: his constantly blaring television was driving her bonkers; he dreamed of ensconcing himself in a secluded space where her hair dryer and phone conversations would be inaudible. They both imagined a fresh take on married life, where they'd be free from their spatially exacerbated

OPPOSITE
This room is epitomized by citrus enthusiasm. A lava stone tabletop and the adjoining room's grass-cloth walls are a saturated and shocking acid yellow green. Such a provocative color is best balanced by a lot of clean white and spiced with accent colors of lemon and lime zest, here in a junk-store light fixture, plates, and vintage needlepoint pillows. The white faux-leather banquette stands up to kid and food combat.

pale vista 2029-60

potpourri green 2029-50

stem green 2029-40

rosemary green 2029-30

My Favorite Contrasts

- Shiny and sleek against matte and casual: mirror with felt . . . Lucite on sisal . . . wood versus plastic

- Three-dimensional versus smooth: grass-cloth- or burlap-covered walls playing off waxed plaster or lacquer walls, leather off linen

- Vintage or antique accessories and furniture paired with modern objects and art: old farm-stand signs hung alongside contemporary black-and-white illustrations or classical etchings . . . a painted pine country table with bright 1960s molded plastic chairs

- Geometrics with organic forms: a set of square glass-and-brass nesting tables next to a bergère chair . . . two black-and-white photographs framed in square matte black frames flanking an ornate French eighteenth-century gilt mirror

OPPOSITE
From a handful of seashells and swatches a master bedroom takes shape.

pet peeves. In their new apartment in New York City, the couple designated a third bedroom as his "man room" for immersion in Sunday golf and miscellaneous cigar pleasure.

The husband did not feel the need to go for a predictably male library or den palette of forest greens, dark reds, and brown leather. Indeed, this Palm Beach native wanted to bring a bit of Florida spirit to his urban enclave. And since the room could be viewed from the public spaces in the apartment, his wife asked that the room still feel "pretty" and part of their home's larger scheme, which was colorful and somewhat feminine. He liked color and pattern as long as it wasn't "ditsy," so we brought in a bold blue-and-green floral print on the furniture and kept the walls a texturally rich cream-colored grass cloth with blue underlining. Their adjacent living room has a large pattern on the walls, but we kept the colors to the same rich cream and black, so there was no color conflict between the two spaces. Purple accent pillows and throws in the living room were a nonliteral reference to the intense blue in the TV room.

In my newlyweds' smallish "man room," we put the television opposite a down-filled sofa, which sat against the wall under a window. We embedded the depth of the flat screen (though called flat, the screens are usually about 5 inches deep) and the larger AV components in the lower recesses claimed from an abutting hall closet. My 6 foot 2 client needed a long sofa so he could watch TV while lying down, but the room was narrow, so we maximized sofa length and skimped on the size of end tables. To save money, I relacquered his red Parsons-style coffee table in a deep blue. I put castors on his old club chair so it could be moved around easily and upholstered it in the same fabric as the sofa to coordinate the two. Walls and curtains were in neutral honey or cream with tiny blue accents in the curtain trim, which also peeked through as the background color below the natural grass-cloth wallpaper.

THIS PAGE AND OPPOSITE
A husband's navy blue and green TV room/den opens through French doors to a more formal black and cream living room. The similar scale and contrasting placement of the patterns in each room (on the walls in the living room and on the furniture in the den) allow for an easy transition.

*Don't let a fear of
being tacky render
you tasteless.*

A bright, fresh family sunroom
in Florida opens to a kitchen
behind. We used white outdoor
fabric on the sofa in a nod to
the three children who inhabit
the space. While there are
many textures in this room—
glass, faux tortoise, embroidery, needlepoint, ceramic,
wicker, grass cloth, sea grass,
painted turned wood, and
painted metal—they are
unified through a regimented
color palatte of whites, blues,
and greens.

Be Precise

Say the word *green* to the man in the fabric store and you may end up being shown a lime or Starbucks tone (also known as bank green), when you really had avocado in mind. I use a Pantone color swatch to guarantee accuracy, but if you do not have access to this product, when you visit the paint or fabric store, bring along a color reference—a paint chip, a picture of a color from a magazine, or a photograph of a sunset that perfectly captures the pinky orange you want for your kitchen wall.

Temper Complementary Colors

Used together, shades that sit opposite each other on a color wheel—red and green, purple and yellow, orange and blue—give rooms vitality. To maximize a combination's potential, use one in its pure form and the other in a muted shade. There is no such thing as an ugly color, only ugly combinations. Colors go wrong when there is no balance or variation in power. Electric green with electric orange—both high voltage and opposite each other on the color wheel—provides too much impact. (Electric green and dull orange is still extremely confrontational but at least balanced.) Pale pink with pale green may look anemic, so gentle and delicate that it can be almost infantile; pale pink with a deep grass green may carry the preppy flag, but at least it is playfully assertive. Pair a bright yellow sofa with heather purple pillows or flank a secretary desk painted glossy orange with side chairs in dusky gray blue.

Avoid overcommon trends. The embrace of good design by mass retailing has brought good aesthetics to more people than ever, but, like a catchy song on Top-40 rotation, the commercial machine can leach the spirit out of charming color combinations by plastering them everywhere. When manufacturers overuse a combination, it loses its potency. Rooms based on them feel very familiar in an unwanted way—the ubiquity of these combos guarantees you'll get sick of them quickly. You know them: wasabi or sea-grass green, cream, chocolate brown, and dark orange all predictably paired in geometric prints or thick stripes, or the cool blues and browns that are great for a beach rental or a dorm room.

The regal gold-and-red palette may look impressive in hotel and condo lobbies, but for long-term living it bears the heavy burden of being a cliché. Everyone has seen these combinations hundreds of times in ads, catalogs, and showrooms. If you work them into your décor, your friends might suspect you of kit shopping.

No stranger to the tides of popular color current running through the fashion world, I'm currently finding myself drawn to gray (which I use as an alternative to beige) in tones from charcoal to palest dove gray that looks almost lilac, and to purples such as plum, aubergine, and raisin. Lately, as a strong counterpoint I'm also using bright acidic yellows and semiprecious jewel tones of peridot, amethyst, and citrine. I can't predict what color usages will come to define the next fifteen years, but I'm willing to bet gray is for the next decade what brown was for the last.

Neutralize. Don't mix two undiluted primary colors in one room. When used in close proximity, red, bright blue, and yellow can make a room visually noisy and primitive. Instead, pair these intense colors with a neutral for sophistication and serenity. For example, consider dark red with chocolate brown, midnight blue with creamy beige, or lemon yellow with soft white.

OPPOSITE, CLOCKWISE FROM ABOVE LEFT
This is an example of colors that sit opposite each other on the color wheel, cool blues and warm oranges, and how well they suit each other; a medium yellow with accents of much brighter yellow and several related tones of green create a tonal living room, but the black painting by Cathy Zuill and dark floors ground the room; the blue living room is an example of how pattern variations, not spectrums of color, can create the "frisson" in a room.

Reconsider what color means. I often hear people say they don't like color . . . but what they really mean is that they do not like bold or primary colors. Neutral palettes are not colorless—pale or light hues have impact and life. Soft shades can create a serene mood without being bland.

Vary surface quality. If you are going to use a lot of pure colors together in a room, vary the texture and sheen to add visual interest and to allow your eye to perceive a variety of depths. You can take advantage of these levels to make the room more dynamic. Painted surfaces should be a contrasting mix of glossy, matte, and weathered finishes. Side tables and chairs, bureaus, and desks in Lucite, metal, lacquer, or even plastic can express the same color in different ways. Stone, glass, leather, and ceramic accessories and architectural details in one color can offset linen, wool, and silk upholstery in a similar shade because the variation in texture is highlighted when they share a hue.

Clash colors carefully. Conflict in color can be an asset, if used with confidence and in broad strokes. For instance, pairing pinks with reds and navy with blacks can be invigorating if you do it with conviction and savvy. Team them with a clean white to act as referee restraining the intensity of the clash. For example, bright white moldings, white marble tabletops, and well-placed white side tables can frame and tame the energy of a room that is elsewhere frantic with bold color.

Be careful with white. It is tempting to be sloppy with white and to treat it as a default background, but many shades of white exist, and they should be chosen deliberately. White, which in the light spectrum actually represents the use of all colors blending together at once, is an active and sometimes even dangerous choice. It must be integrated thoughtfully because of its ability to punctuate. In the absence of other colors, white loses its power and becomes merely a quality of light or an overwhelmingly dull backdrop. In a white room, anything that is *not* white will necessarily steal the show, no matter how subtle its color. This includes plants, artwork, or a wooden floor. There can be no afterthought in a white room; everything takes on import and significance. Because the non-white accoutrements are going to grandstand in such a stark setting, select them carefully; they should be worthy of attention.

Most rooms require some white or off-white to create continuity of mood. In its different tones, it can be crisp and cool or very warm. Unless it is your intention to work the spectrum, pick a white and stick with it to accent the interplay of your other color choices. I often find myself repainting ceilings, doors, or trim that are in otherwise good condition because they were painted in standard-issue superwhite that doesn't work well with the common creamier or grayer whites in the background of the fabric or wallpaper the client is using.

Use black with deliberation. Black is an incredibly powerful color choice and terribly hard to paint over! If you are working with black as an accent, give serious thought to where the black elements should go—and try to distribute them evenly around the space. Unless the black highlights carry the eye from place to place on purpose, they can overpunctuate a particular area of the room. If you have one black item you like, add two more for balance, and separate them. A black border in your rug benefits from the presence of a black lacquered chest on a shelf or black legs on a secretary. Black picture frames can be balanced by a black pillow, lampshade, or elements in the trim on a drapery.

OPPOSITE

This vivid turquoise blue vitrine display cabinet is matched by the orange grass cloth and bright white chair— we wanted to show the shapes of the furniture, and the use of color allows the silhouettes to take center stage.

LEFT

A breakfast nook took its cues from the record collection below, where blue-gray and newsprint colors predominate. A pillow and photography add a flare of color to this cool palette that reads almost like a photographer's negative.

ABOVE
These two rooms illustrate using white with care. The cream, chocolate brown, black, and white bedroom, left, is a study in color balance. The black lampshades and cabinets on either side of the room keep the space from being a total creampuff. On the right, a high-traffic living room's whites are in durable finishes, as are the lava stone cocktail table, painted floors, and lacquer side tables. The navy blue mohair sofa and faux leather wing chair will stand up to everyday abuse.

OPPOSITE
Pattern, texture, and sheen, not architecture, define this entryway library in a large Tribeca loft. The vignette includes a floor stained in two colors and then painted to create an inlay pattern. We combined earthy organic elements with very glam finishes and mid-century austerity in part achieved with subtle cream (chairs), bronze (cocktail table), and shagreen (faux leather–lined bookcases).

Tone down bold patterns. When using bold fabric patterns, choose tonal combinations. Light and dark shades of the same color in a pattern will balance the oomph of the graphic.

Employ gradation. Create a unique ombré effect on walls with white trim and ceiling by starting with a dark color at the base moldings and softly blending in more white to cover the wall with progressively lighter shades as you move upward. A subtle spectrum of color washes up the surface, elongating the wall and giving lift to the ceiling, which can then be painted in an even lighter tone of the same color.

Textural Matters

Where color can't play the role of headline accessory, pattern and sheen can. A small foyer belonging to a very fashion-forward couple presented a tough challenge. They wanted a lot of pizzazz, but due to size constraints, the space couldn't hold much furniture. Because it opened into three other rooms, we couldn't employ a dominant color that would dictate or conflict with the other schemes. We had already selected a brilliant blue wallpaper with a large-scale pattern for their adjoining living room, so we decided to pick up the pattern cues from that wallpaper and use the ebonized floor as our canvas for a spread of oversized floral shapes in white and gold. Mirroring the deep glossy black on the floor is a black faux patent-leather ceiling. This liquid black sky transformed the tiny square of a foyer into an important entrance and disproved that design adage "a dark ceiling always lowers the ceiling's height."

With such a bold floor and ceiling, we had to take a quieter stance with the walls, but they still needed to hold their own. We painted them white, but to add interest we created a vertical stripe pattern of contrasting sheens. We alternated 6 inches of matte-finish white and 10 inches of high-gloss finish in the same shade. These stripes traveled around the entry and down the lengths of the two adjoining halls. The effect was not quite as strong as I had hoped

OPPOSITE AND ABOVE
A careful interplay of materials and color gives these two rooms variety and identity, but in a cohesive fashion—important because they open to each other.

for, however, so I added a thin gold accent line. This served to further delineate the stripes but keep them subtle and neutral enough so that they didn't detract from the artwork.

Texture (matte, gloss, metallic) is as important as color. Everything has a yin and a yang, and that's what texture in a room is all about, a balance of feel and scale. Pleasing juxtapositions of a wide spectrum of items give rooms velocity or energetic movement, volume, and va-va-va-voom. You can most appreciate a piece when it is in contrast to something else. A tree stump is just a tree stump until it is placed next to a club chair—it then becomes an ironic statement, a strong silhouette, and possibly a useful footrest.

I used a vintage mirror with white trim in the dining room so that it would reflect the blue wallpaper from the living room like a painting on the yellow walls of the dining room. In turn, the mirror in the living room adds a big splash of yellow from the dining room.

The late British designer David Hicks drew rooms with symmetry but injected a feeling of novelty by juxtaposing classic pieces with contemporary ones. He would cover antique French chairs with bold, graphic fabric, place an ancient urn near an ultramodern abstract painting, and plop an antique bronze bust atop a Lucite column. Tall next to short, matte with shiny, willowy by stumpy, natural mixed with artificial, glam and rudimentary, elemental meshed with formal. All these combinations create new ways for your belongings to communicate.

My client couple who worked in the fashion and music businesses wanted a lot of *pow* via pattern and texture in their living room. To contrast with the staid and plump sofa in navy mohair he bought, I recovered a pair of his uncle's old vertically channeled wing chairs. They harnessed a whimsical Austin Powers sensibility that I played up by recovering the seats in gold faux leather and lacquering the curvaceous legs in a glossy gray. We painted the floor a bright white because the walls were medium to dark.

In Praise of Faux Leather

I love covering walls with faux leather that has been either upholstered or simply glued flat to the wall. Imitation hide is an especially effective treatment for small rooms because it acts as a luxe-defining feature without taking up floor space. In any-sized room, faux animal skin adds drama and texture. It can be very traditional (caramel calf with nail-head details or a patinated, tufted chocolate cowhide) or ultramodern (bright colors or metallic finishes, or exotic skins such as shagreen, python, ostrich leg, or stitched eel). With a menu of creatures like that, I begin to get squeamish and have a crisis of confidence, so almost always opt for faux leather.

Another advantage is its ease of availability and consistency in large quantities, which is always such a problem with natural skins. Nearly unlimited color options and slightly interpretive patterns are another benefit of faux skin. For instance, in my line of faux leathers for Valtekz, I like to take out the tapering of a genuine snake pattern because it reminds me, on an instinctual level, of the fangs and shaking tails. I make the patterning a bit more abstract than the real thing—playing with the best of nature.

Animal hides are difficult, expensive, and environmentally toxic to dye well. Despite the highly developed crafts of tanning and dyeing, it remains a challenge to get a pure white or a light pastel on a natural product without the scars, pimples, and bug bites of real skin showing. With new leather, some of which is vulnerable to heat, sun, and water damage, the first scratches or greasy stain and smudge have none of the appeal they do on an old leather, where such accidents are layered (and well earned) over time. Some have a built-in patina of age, beautifully rendered and ready to go. Antique leather that has earned a century-old patina is a beautiful thing, but in the real world that aging process is long, arduous, and ugly.

Material Matters

I try to include at least one of each of these textures in some form or another in every room I design:

Linen—charming with its rumples when washed; it hangs with laid-back insouciance.

Velvet, silk velvet, or mohair—best for showing off gently curved shapes in upholstery, and also a source of deep pigment and warmth.

Felt—soft, muted, and matte textured. This very unassuming fabric carries a lot of power and shows off great tailoring.

Embroidery, crewelwork, or needlepoint—has a vintage or homespun quality due to its stitchery.

Hemp, raffia, or burlap—earthy, sturdy, and casual.

Grass cloth—natural, breathable. Works as both organic and glam due to its subtle sheen.

Silk—elegant, crisp; another fabric that holds color pigments fabulously.

Crisp cotton—playful, easy, fun, soft. Often the source of print or geometric pattern in a room.

Wood—warm, versatile. Preferably some dry, unfinished wood, some painted, and some in a beautiful hand rubbed finish, either waxed or French polished.

Tole—old painted metal lampshades, frames, and boxes. A wonderful alternative to lacquered elements, it adds a vintage feel.

Mirror—light, bright, brilliant, and glam or heathered and moody as it slides down the scale to antique.

Lucite—sleek, simultaneously contemporary and retro, fashionable.

Lacquer—lustrous; lends easy jolts of color.

Sheer textiles—moody, soft, willowy; softens direct sunlight.

Shell, horn, bone—smooth, with layers of natural sheen.

Animal prints—impart a sense of energy and fun, especially in traditional rooms.

Leather or faux leather—practical, natural texture that plays off formal materials like velvet and silk.

Ikat—earthy, ethnic flair, especially when used on classic forms like wing chairs.

Suzani—embroidery adds texture and color.

To keep it cozy for bare feet and cold winters, and to temper the myriad surrounding colors and pattern, I laid a large solid gray wool area rug on top. Because we had a solid-color, hulking-in-scale sofa and some theatrically comedic chairs, we chose a coffee table that was skeletally clean lined and very elegant. It was as lean and absent as the sofa was squishily present. The crackle-glazed lava-stone top on the table proved a practical and durable (no way to hurt this lab-tested surface) injection of bright white.

I am partial to colorful and comfortable rooms, natural fabrics, lots of texture, and dramatic furniture forms. And I like to add a smattering of glam through accents like mirrors, Lucite, and metallic furniture mixed with the rustic feel of heavily patinated finishes. But these touches are blended with traditional design staples of the last seventy years—custom-upholstered Bridgewater-arm skirted sofas, printed fabrics, abundant throw pillows, and collected or found older pieces—to produce an overall effect of reassuring solidity and livable comfort.

Ultimately, the best and most tasteful design schemes are those that articulate individuality. I look for intimacy and thoughtfulness in a home, not necessarily grandeur or rigid interpretation of rules. I do not need rooms to be formal but they should be distinctive. And finally, character can trump all rules—as long as it is conveyed with sensibility, honesty, and restraint, a room is in good taste.

OPPOSITE
TOP ROW: *Glass beaded wallpaper; Lucite leg; crystal towel holder; mosaic glass tiles.*
SECOND ROW: *Lucite curtain pole with bronze rings; antique mirrors; textured fabrics; silk fabric with hand-blocked wallpaper.*
THIRD ROW: *Finish samples in lacquered grass cloth, faux tortoise, and zebrano wood; wax plaster over decorative relief pattern; capize shell wallpaper, patinated silver metal, and metallic leather; black and red sisal with black and red marble.*
BOTTOM ROW: *Amethyst tabletop; color palette for ceramic tile; satin and sea grass; and rock crystal doorknobs.*

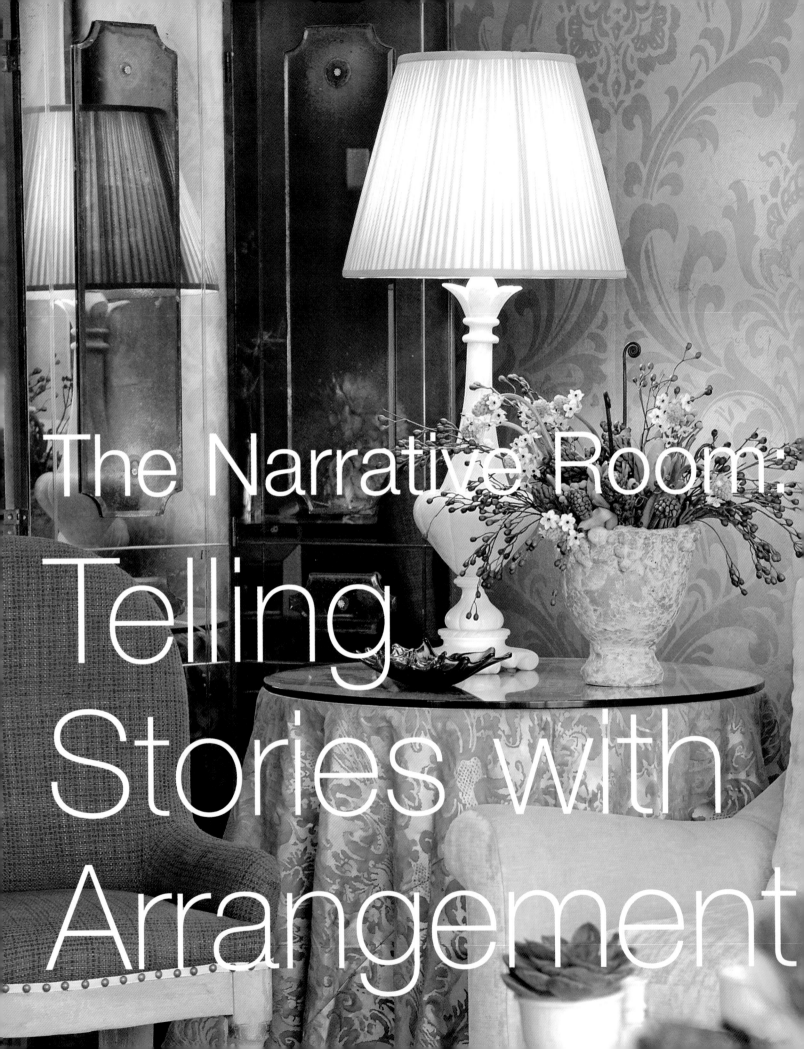

The Narrative Room: Telling Stories with Arrangement

You can pay tribute to your room's finest features through smart and sensitive arrangement of furniture and accessories. To do this you'll resolve practical, aesthetic, and personal issues: Is there a view you want to contemplate or show off? Furnishings should not only be oriented toward the window; they should frame it as well. Will you take meals in the room? Consider stowaway folding trays or an extralarge, slightly higher coffee table for a more comfortable living/eating combination. Do children and pets play in the space? Durably upholstered or finished furniture should be readily accessible (even if you have to pull it out from a corner or closet) so small family members and other creatures can join in and have their fun, too. Before you begin shopping, consider lifestyle points as well: Do your rooms need to be easily rearranged for multiple purposes? Does clutter make you crazy or comfort you?

Once you start putting together the pieces, you can create a narrative by applying a few rules. You want to create enough of a feeling of repose so that the room's energy doesn't exhaust you. For instance, a room overloaded with objects on the same plane dulls your visual sense. Exploit multiple heights, giving your eyes respite and diversity as they dance around. Your eye will happily travel from a stately étagère to a glassed-in bookcase, to a secretary, tree, screen, or row of still art hung high; then to lamps on tables, sofa and chair backs at a middle elevation, and ultimately to low ottomans and jolts of color coming from the rug on the floor or from a beautiful ceramic cachepot holding a lush green plant. Tuck unexpected sculptural items in surprise locations. In our house a ceramic dog sits under the piano, and a few pieces of art hang unusually low above small stools.

Choose color, fabric, and furnishings to meet your living priorities as well as your room's idiosyncrasies, flaws, and features. Family-oriented houses will require additional attention to mess management and delineation of parent privacy and child play areas. How many people do you intend to have in the room most of the time? What are the frequency, size, and style of your parties if you throw them? Will guests spend most of their time standing because you have cocktail parties, or seated, because you entertain in a more intimate or meal-focused way? Plan for lots of smaller conversational seating areas in cocktail-party rooms, and "free" areas for milling around and walking. Are these larger meals frequent enough so that you must design for them to happen often, or merely for occasional adaptability? How many children do you have living in the house? How old are they? Are their friends welcome?

If the idea of precise floor plans intimidates you, start with a hybrid I call the photo elevation. You will, at some point, need to draw or otherwise procure precisely scaled room measurements. But such accuracy isn't necessary when you're jump-starting the creative process. First, play with possible layout compositions. Crouch in the middle of each room and take a picture in the direction of each wall from about 3 feet high, so you have both the foreground of the floor and the ceiling molding in the shot.

Print the images in full on an 8-by-10 piece of paper and then use an overlay of tracing paper to sketch furniture pieces (roughly to scale if you can. I draw a faint line around the room at "34 inches" on my photo so that furniture differences can be seen from that height). You will end up with a scratch-pad rendering of how the space could look—not as the crow flies (which is what a plan represents) but with furniture viewed frontally as you will see it in real life. You'll also be able to make note of the blank canvas walls, and draw in curtain treatments and potential wall art as well.

OPPOSITE
A mix of rustic and traditional defines this sitting room/garden room— classic bergère chairs have a casual air with a time-weathered finish and burlap striped fabric. The large potted plants in the window sit on an outdoor garden stand, creating a haphazard greenhouse effect in the room.

The cozy sitting room has three seating areas and there is something of interest at every level, from a colorful patterned rug on the floor to floral-topped trays on midlevel ottomans, to a full, high bookcase and goblet-pleated curtains at the room's highest points.

As you solidify your designs, you will need to develop an accurate floor plan and insert the exact scale measurements of your chosen furniture pieces so you can be sure that the arrangements you've created actually work with the physical measurements of your room. I recommend enlisting the help of a friend to make accurate measurements. Use graph paper to carefully draw the measurements of the walls, doors, and windows—and place all architectural features accurately. I emphatically urge you to do this in ½-inch scale, and to do it very carefully. Do not measure wall to wall, but from the base molding on one side to the base molding on the other. Moldings may cost you as much as a 3-inch shrinkage in your available floor space. For apartment dwellers and those measuring for rugs, the small loss is a big deal. Also, remember to measure from the front of the hearth (which usually subtracts about 18 inches from a wall-to-wall measurement on a real estate developer's floor plan) if you have a fireplace.

Make copies of your plan drawing before you place the furniture on it so you have extras to experiment with. Use tracing paper layers and drafts to tinker with the layout. While ½-inch

In this chaotically warm, English-inspired library, the volume and plethora of objects, ornament, and rich color defines the room as cozy and inviting.

scale drawing is a hassle (as opposed to the common kit of ¼-inch cutouts or magnetic plans), it is important because the mere width of a pencil line on a ¼-inch scale can represent an inch or more of error. In ¼-inch scale, by the time you add up the implications of a smidge here and a smudge there, the errors can accumulate into magnitude of feet. When your rug arrives three months later, it might climb up the edges of walls; your end tables might sidestep into doorways, and your sofa and chair arms could end up kissing in cramped quarters.

If you are starting with a "blank canvas" (or one where you plan to change only floors and wall treatment or color), sand and stain the floor (if it is wood) but leave off the top sealant coat and protect the floor with drop cloths until the rest of the work is done. Prime the walls and trim first (a skim coat is ideal, though more expensive), then paint, paper, or upholster the walls. If you paint before laying wall-to-wall carpet, leave off the final coat on the base molding's trim until the rug goes down. The moldings will suffer some abuse during the rug installation, but it's good to have the paint applied first so that if it's a high-pile rug, you don't have to worry about angling a brush behind it to reach the floor base.

Unless I plan to expose the floor completely (which I tend to do only in hallways or dining rooms), I like to cover as much as I can with one large area rug that fills the room up to 9 or 18 inches off the walls. This defines the room and makes it cozier. Beautiful wood will still make its impact in the border areas. The smaller you make the rug, the smaller the room feels. Floor areas outside the rug become peripheral to the heart of the room, taking on a border-zone feel. (By the way, the same principle applies to stair runners—I like to go as wide as possible.) An oversized and relatively inexpensive sisal rug handles the problem of small budget meets big, empty space.

When buying a large rug, try to find one that has a flat enough pile to allow for a second, smaller rug to be placed on top. To set apart a special seating group, this secondary rug can be centered beneath the sofa and coffee table. All sisals except the ropey-thick jute or abaca versions are suitable to carry decorative top rugs. Like an attention-getting scarf atop a simple outfit, this smaller rug can supply luxurious materials and construction, high-impact color, or antique provenance that, at full room scale, would cost a fortune.

After you've laid down floor coverings, place the largest pieces of furniture first. In a living room, this is most often the sofa (even though I've recommended that you actually choose other items first); in a bedroom, the bed. Smaller pieces will be arranged around them. You do not have to cram the entire seating area on top of the secondary rug like a beach party sharing a towel—the sofa can be just on the edge of it, or just off it. Large chairs (not occasional seating) are allowed to straddle; two legs on, two off.

When it comes to finding items in a pleasing scale, I'm partial to vintage furniture and antiques because furniture made decades ago (and even older than that) was often built on a smaller, more intimate but still serviceable scale. These pieces manage to achieve comfort without being as bulky as a lot of the new furniture for sale today. There is something down-market and very, very 1980s about huge "overstuffed" furniture pieces. We jettisoned enormous shoulder pads twenty years ago (though they try, occasionally, to make a comeback) but the steroidal effect has stuck it out in couches, armchairs, and upholstered dining chairs for reasons I can't explain. Though it does seem to sell to a broader market, greater size does not necessarily translate into greater comfort. Coziness can be achieved with a 37-inch-deep sofa. (That's shallower than many of today's supersized sofas, which commonly stretch in depth from 40 to 46 inches.) Comfort is driven by the pitch and angle of the back, the construction and fill of the cushions. The only depth that matters is that of the interior seat, which shouldn't fall short of 22 inches.

Place a coffee table in reachable proximity to the sofa—but not too close. On a floor plan I like to leave 15 inches on all sides, but comfort and personal preference will dictate what's right for you once you are seated. Then arrange the chairs that go around the table. Try to match the scale of the key elements, a sofa and two club chairs. I like having pairs of chairs, but in a small space a love seat and one club chair of similar style work. From there you can decide if you can sustain (or fit) two club chairs and two more small-frame decorative chairs to go along with them—such as bergère or shield-back armchairs (armless if you are really tight on space). The fabric on the wood-framed chairs should complement but not match the upholstery on the sofa and club chairs; you might want to have them upholstered in a fabric that you love but that must be used sparingly either because it's delicate or expensive.

Place one side table on either end of the sofa and a very small one in between any pair of chairs, or next to a single seat. Having a flat surface next to every chair ensures that no one has to reach too far to set down his or her drink or book, and creates a nice tier effect. Have fun with something as simple or whimsical as a two-tier vintage phone table or a tree stump. An upturned 18-inch high glass vase or a small metal plant stand can even suffice. I prefer side tables that are an inch or two lower than where your arm falls in the chair or sofa arm.

OPPOSITE
I set apart a small dining nook in a Manhattan apartment from the rest of the room by the curtain treatment and the Aleman Moore colorful straw rug placed atop the loft-like living room's wall-to-wall sea-grass carpet.

The Measure of a Meal

Table and seating height, and the spacing around dining furniture, are nonnegotiable. It is amazing how just 1 inch in such a familiar ratio as chair-to-table height can seem Alice-in-Wonderland off-kilter. The following height standards have been set for years: The conventional table height for dining comfortably is 29 inches, but can go to 31 inches if your chairs' seats are higher than 18 inches. You want 12 inches from the top of the seat of your chair to the bottom of your table. Less than 10 inches for the gap from top of chair seat to bottom of table will be knee-knockingly uncomfortable for anyone who tries to cross his or her legs. You can fudge it with odd, untraditional, or old pieces, if necessary, by having a professional carpenter make simple adjustments like installing casters to add height or trimming table or chair legs to subtract it.

Having enough space behind dining chairs is also essential for comfort. Allow 3 feet because it takes 2 feet to pull out the chair and 1 to stand behind it. If your dining room is small, or serves double duty as a reading room or an office, consider a banquette. I use them often, even when space is not a consideration, because I like the juxtaposition of generous upholstery against the cleaner architecture of the table. They are flexible, too (you can always squeeze in an extra person).

For dining tables, the choice of shape is pretty personal. I prefer round or oval for the sheer democracy they offer as well as their ability to equitably and comfortably accommodate crammed-in extras. Squares and rectangles have corners—and being seated at one is a form of social punishment; sight lines and conversation are dramatically compromised for the corner-bound, cutting them out of the discussion. When calculating the absolute minimum space per person, you will need no less than 25 inches of personal space, the elbow-to-elbow width of the average person.

For one couple in New York who weren't really sure about what to do with their dining room, I used a round pedestal table with a banquette and lightweight chairs they could pull up for a fun night of cocktails or a card game, as well as for the rarer formal dinner. Two small side tables served as a bar. When another couple, tight on space, confessed that they weren't the kind of people who threw formal dinners or, for that matter, sat down often to dinner at the dining table at all, I scrapped the entire dining room and turned it into a screening room. In a corner of their living room, I placed a 40-inch round table (around which they could cram six people if they really wanted to) with a small modular banquette making an otherwise "lost" space look important *and* giving them a place to eat when they'd had enough of the coffee table or kitchen—or really wanted to entertain guests in a more formal setting.

These little stands are very important in contributing a leggy or varied contour if all the upholstery in the room is skirted or falls to the floor. Conversely, if everything in the room is leggy, you can have the tiny table skirted to the floor for contrast or you can use a small trunk for ballast. Balancing the spindly and the stocky is key—variety always looks more interesting than matching sets. Lots of wooden legs everywhere leave a room with a skittish air (I always think of a herd of gazelles primed to flee from a predator) while too many skirts or low-weighted furniture pieces feel heavy and lumbering.

Once you have arranged the room, live with it for a while and see how comfortable and welcome the arrangement makes you feel. Can you move around it easily? Does it accommodate all of the room's various uses? If it's not working in real life, move tables and chairs, swap sofa and chair pillows, or switch out one coffee table for another (another good reason to save receipts). Give it time. But don't let holes in your plan stop you from progressing, either. The blank portion of a wall will eventually be filled with the perfect secretary or étagère; the ideal piece of art for the mantel appears when you least expect it. Flawless room arrangements do not have to materialize in a day, or remain the same in perpetuity.

BELOW
The branches have been left on a wooden beam in this country cabin bathroom— allowing a perch for a stuffed quail and a makeshift robe hook.

Adding Ornament

Though accessories are the least functionally essential elements in a room, they have great power to add personality and character. When placed properly, these objects help us "register" a room's spirit because they lead the eye to rest on a particular focal point. They also convey a message about the room (formality, whimsy, art, books). And for the owner, they are a pleasure to change, update, improve, contract, or expand over time. You can take chances with accessories since they are easily moved, hidden, and replaced. Remember, they don't all have to be out at once. That's what cupboards are for.

The fact that you can break rules with accessories doesn't justify mayhem. Train yourself to edit, edit, edit. The difference between a humble display of junk and a collection of interesting objects often comes down to the manner of display. Your own assurance that an object is worth admiring can make it so. Highlight what you choose to put on view. If it's in a bookcase, turn the back wall into a dramatic backdrop. Mirror it, wallpaper it in a small-scale pattern, paint it a contrasting color, or upholster it in velvet or leather. Then light it all up—train a spot on it from the ceiling, put lights in the shelf's casing, or use wall-mounted picture lights to illuminate it.

A good art collection need not be only expensive pieces from the top Chelsea galleries. My own walls showcase the detritus of flea markets and hand-me-downs, with the scrawls of good friends mixed in. At a cocktail party recently, a professional art consultant (who shall remain nameless) began to hold forth kindly but pretentiously on our "magnificent collection." She asked me about the background of each piece and her face deflated as we revealed the actual

provenance. Little of it met her standards of legitimacy. If our apartment were going up in flames, I might fight my way back in to retrieve our most revered piece, a science-classroom relic that depicts the dominant and recessive genetic characteristics of mating guinea pigs.

If you have freestanding objects, group them in glass boxes or under glass globes, the kinds once used to encase clocks or ripening melons. When you display every knickknack and vase, the dusting and cleaning turns into a nightmare. Many of us, myself included, keep things that become beloved over time. A few years ago in Palm Beach my mother heard the fire alarm calling for an emergency edit when a friend cracked, "You have more stuff here than TGI Friday's." When he asked, "How in the world do you manage the dusting?" my mom responded, "I just turn up the fans."

The art of grouping objects requires judicious restraint. For example, people often have too many different kinds of picture frames. Warring styles of frames distract the eye from the real stars, the actual photos or artwork, which more or less defeats the point of showing them in the first place. Instead, use frames that are of a similar look or material such as all Lucite, bamboo, or silver. If there is one piece you really want to play up, by all means set it apart by framing it distinctly. But this only works if the others are more uniform.

Grouping by color or form can also keep the feeling of object anarchy at bay. When we selected our wedding-table setting, my husband wanted multicolored wineglasses. Because we already had a jumble of china patterns and silverware, I was fixated on purchasing a matching set of crystal with our wedding registry credit. We fought briefly but ultimately compromised by buying the glasses from a variety of manufacturers but all in the same shade of green. They had differing decorative details, shapes, and heights, which turned out to be more interesting than a boxed set, but the common color gave our table a semblance of unity. We are both much happier because our "collection" represents our love of variety and of the individual object.

When arranging a console, coffee, or side table, think about where you need height and color; look around and see where those elements are lacking and add them to a tabletop. Perhaps

ABOVE LEFT
Simple metal stands raise vintage eyeglass molds to sculptural prominence.

ABOVE
Three accessories adorn a mantelpiece, connected by their circular form: a cloudy mirror, an antique clock, and a ceramic plate.

OPPOSITE
A modern glass vase provides a counterpoint to traditional wallpaper.

OVERLEAF
The main furniture and fabrics in this bedroom are in an ethereal pale aqua. For restrained contrast in the rugs, painted wood furniture, and fabrics, we used white and cream. Because the palette is so subtle, most accessories were chosen in Lucite, silver leaf, or platinum hammered metal to offer glamorous glimmer without distracting from the room's serenity.

you need color over in a dark corner. Or, if all your furniture is new, some vintage relief can come from a heavily patinated object placed on a side table. A ceramic object, a basket, a painting on an easel, or a Lucite or stone sculpture may be just the thing. Be wary of overloading the coffee table. It is a bad place for stationary clutter. Leave it empty except for flowers, large-scale books, and perhaps a tray. Consider putting a box or tray *under* the table to hide necessities—remote controls, notepads, and pens. Or find a table with a built-in undershelf if you're concerned about kicking the box across the room every time you sit down.

Mirrors are multipurpose, especially useful accessories—they work as space enhancements, indirect light sources, and as an instrument through which other rooms can be made visible. They bring color into a room by reflecting it from an adjoining space. Hang a framed mirror instead of art on one wall or install ¼-inch sheet mirror directly to the wall from molding to molding.

Artwork is a powerful element in overall room design, but the choice of which art to show is one I usually leave to my clients, many of whom have strong ideas about artwork or are collectors in their own right. At any rate, I can't fairly call art an accessory. Taste in art is so highly personal that I urge most of my clients to search for their acquisitions over a long stretch of time. Paintings, photographs, drawings, or sculpture get chosen after my role in the room is mostly finished. I always hope my clients will shop on their own to find pieces that speak to the space (and to them) and offer an important contribution to its ongoing conversation. As I

THIS PAGE, CLOCKWISE
FROM ABOVE LEFT
*An eclectic mix of objects
becomes sculpturally
interesting because of their
placement on this machin-
ist's rack in a Tribeca
apartment; blue-and-white
china and a bowl of walnuts
sit on top of a red lacquered
telephone table next to a
slipper chair upholstered in
a cut-silk velvet pattern;
in my own apartment, a
nineteenth-century cam-
paign bench upholstered in
a graphic pattern sits below
two of my most favorite
objects, a framed scroll—an
educational tool to demon-
strate the dominant and
recessive traits of mating
guinea pigs—and a jury-
rigged melon cloche sus-
pended from an adjustable
pivot mechanism.*

Framed

- In modern settings, consider white frames instead of black; black can create too pronounced an outline and detract from the image.
- Use different depths and widths of frames in the same color and finish for subtle variety. For a quick room cleanup, paint all your frames the same color.
- If you don't have large-scale art, buy small items in multiples, or frame a grouping of related subjects in exactly the same style as if they were a set—there is nothing cooler than sixteen prints from a series or ten drawings in the same frames massed together on the wall. They have the impact of one important piece of art.
- Think of the matting as a way to carry color through the room—in a neutral or all-white room, for example, you could matte all pictures with your accent color, say celadon or apricot.

- Enjoy holiday cards and family pictures without cluttering up public spaces or refrigerator doors—we keep our ever-changing array of cards and "snaps" on the inside of the kitchen cabinet doors. We get the joy of seeing them whenever we open them, but they do not visually clutter the kitchen.
- Install panels of corkboard inside a workstation or in the kitchen as a place to pin an ever-revolving display of snapshots, doodles, drawings, and grocery lists.
- Lay a framed piece leaning against the wall on a bureau or table. It's easy for the picture to "wander" about your house.
- Hang groups of items that do not need frames, such as plates and porcelain pot lids, directly on the wall and place small sculptures in shadow box frames. If framed or grouped properly, almost any everyday item can be shown or seen in a new light.

shop art fairs and galleries, specific styles of art bring certain clients to mind, and even if it's years later, I'll call them with a recommendation to go look at something that struck me as potentially interesting.

I am not one to match a painting with a color scheme as if it is a lampshade, but I do think it can be extremely important to consider the dialogue between art and its setting. A very large, modern painting in a traditional room can both startle and refresh. A traditional landscape or portrait placed in an ultramodern setting can also be appealing. I like to remove formal paintings from fancy frames and hang them with the bare canvas, stripped of the gilt frame's pomp and circumstance. I think the piece looks more found and less overblown this way—beloved, not curated. (Paint the frame a new color and use it elsewhere or put a mirror in it.)

To create a unique or dramatic look, play with frame scale and matting when you are preparing artwork such as photography, watercolors, and pen-and-ink drawings. You might use a frame that mixes both silver and gold leaf for versatility's sake. Make a small picture appear larger by giving it a large-scale setting—a wide mat and an imposing frame. Hang pictures in front of a bookcase for texture and depth. Or lean pictures inside a bookcase or on top of a chest or against a wall for a casual, haphazard gallery-in-the-works look.

Whatever you add to your room, know that if it doesn't work out, the solution is rather simple: your blunders can be returned, recycled, resold (that's what eBay is for!), or reused in another way or another room. If you're not spending a lot of money, it's better to try out the charming 1960s pottery monkey or the mounted examples of rope knots in your living room than to leave the space looking bare. The biggest mistake is boredom!

OPPOSITE, CLOCKWISE FROM ABOVE LEFT *A vintage gilt and black-painted plastic mirror reflects an antique ceiling fixture and artwork across the room; descending into a playroom, blue-toned large-scale photos of a client's children adorn a green-grass-cloth-covered wall; a hallucinatory-colored mixed-media artwork fills the niche from base molding to ceiling beam in this downtown loft living room/dining room.*

Reality Show: Designing Around Life

Chapter Six

Mirror, Mirror

Mirrors amplify light and brightness in a room. Place a mirror opposite a window to duplicate or double any natural light a room receives. Or place one at the end of a dark hallway or in a forlorn corner.

Finances, schedules, work, spouses, babies, pets, guests, and existing architecture . . . there is a long list of items that can frustrate even the most carefully planned design scheme. With compromise and ingenuity, nearly every decorating dilemma can be eliminated, disguised, or at least accommodated.

Let's get something sensitive out of the way: finances, almost always the first hurdle of any design project. No matter what a person has to spend on a project, it never seems to be enough to do everything he or she wants. At every budget, people face the same challenges. They forget to allow room for errors. Inevitably, they underestimate the cost of labor. In some cases, people experience taste inflation: as they learn more about their options, they start to care more about the quality of details that previously held no interest for them. Beware! Knowledge can be the gateway to financial vice!

People are often so eager to get started that they neglect to account for the eventual impact of unavoidable budget items frequently not in the estimate. The cost of shipping, extended warranties, and sales tax should be an expected percentage of the overall budget, but for some reason, most home owners turn a blind eye to these realities until the final bill. I've seen another kind of budgetary fog blow in when people review contractors' bids. They will accept the optimistic pricing of a low-baller and learn later about all of the "but this"es and "except that"s. Remember, often the contractor with the lowest bid is just serving you the best-case scenario, and the more expensive contractor may be giving you the whole story up front.

Trade-offs and compromise are an inevitable part of the design process. What looks like a large allotment of cash can disappear—and very quickly—because, as described before, rising budgets often lead to rising expectations and material costs. Budget is usually relative to lifestyle requirements, so the person who has, say, $600,000 to $1 million to spend on a design project is looking for a very high degree of service, finish, and quality. For some of my clients, a $35,000 reproduction carpet is a compromise, when the dreamed-of $100,000 antique exceeds their seemingly generous limit. For others, a $900 rug is the breaking point. I can't just pick a paint color and expect the $600,000 client to be happy with painted drywall. For them, a finished wall may involve minor architectural enhancements, wallpapering, and faux finishes, while the client with the $1 million budget might expect custom paneling, wall upholstery, hand-painted murals, and antique wallpapers.

For the great majority of us, who don't have an elastic budget, the elements that go into making a high-impact room inevitably add up, and nothing is as quickly or cheaply achieved as TV home improvement shows imply. When you see a room being "done" for $500 or $1,000, the actual quality of the fabrics and other materials looks better through the filter of the small screen. Market-rate labor costs are rarely calculated in the total. (How often does the good-looking carpenter pop by your house to cheerfully build a new bookcase for free? And when was the last time the chipper closet editor came through to bolster your self-confidence and gently edit your wardrobe just for fun? Or the stylist to prop your bookcases?) These makeover stories usually reflect the unaccounted-for handiwork of many unseen professionals. And the few costs they do track are often discounted for the media exposure.

ABOVE
A highly polished aluminum chest of drawers reflects light throughout a Nantucket guest bedroom.

OPPOSITE
A trellis-patterned plaster-textured wallpaper gives height and color to a staircase that leads to a wine cellar and a media room.

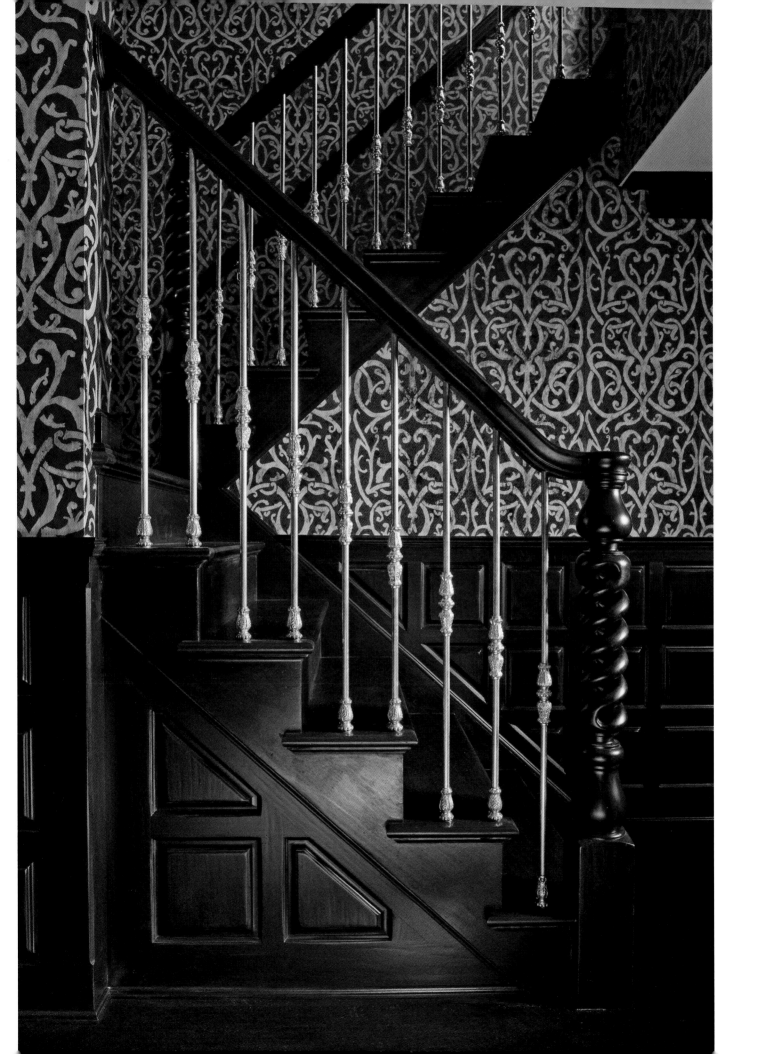

OPPOSITE
The wallpaper in each of these three rooms, which range from a New York apartment to a Florida bedroom to a cabin guest bedroom, provides architectural interest.

Seemingly simple, bare-bones do-it-yourself carpentry jobs have hidden costs attached: tools need to be rented or purchased; time is wasted, frustration expended, and inevitable errors repaired. I don't know about you, but my drill rarely has a full charge, and by the time I can find its power cord, I'm bound to discover the necessary drill bit is the one that's fled the kit.

By way of a common example, I'll warn you to dodge the siren song of off-the-rack floating shelves. With their bewitching simplicity (two or three screws, right?) they promise extra storage and clean, almost sculptural lines for your walls, but they usually offer a snare, i.e. first you must reinforce the wall with plywood or studs, patch, repaint the wall, then install the shelf. Without this preparation, the seemingly inexpensive shelf will most likely carve a large hieroglyph on the wall as it tumbles to the ground under the weight of your now-broken frame or vase, for example.

My intention is not to be defeatist, but to be reasonable. You cannot do too much for too little. However, here are some high-impact approaches you can take to stretch a small budget. If, for example, $5,000 is your allotment, following a few simple steps may result in the greatest change to your lifestyle and look.

The first force for positive change is also the easiest: a good purge. The second is to maintain what you have. Consider using your money to hire a cleaning professional to keep your home in top-notch condition, rather than attempting to reinvent your space wholesale when it is not financially feasible. Get rid of the shabby, the hoarded, the broken, the useless, and the unattractive, and live (probably more happily than you imagined) with what's left. *Antiques Roadshow* is a tease as tempting as the lottery. Just remember you are probably as likely to be eaten by a shark as you are to cash out when those tchotchkes are acquired by the Smithsonian. Try to apply the two-year rule. If you haven't used it in the past twenty-four months, you can live without it forever. If going cold turkey won't fly, waste a bit of money on a few years of storage to ease the pain of separation from your clutter. The lifestyle payoff may be worth it.

You may find this transformation to be all you need, but if you are still hankering for a new look, try step three: investing in a dramatic wall treatment. This may be labor intensive or expensive, but for the concentration of your dollars, it will have the greatest effect on the room overall. In order of escalating price, paint, wallpaper, trompe l'oeil, fabric upholstery (depending on the cost of the fabric), or even full mirroring, will alter the look of your space dramatically. Step four: paint your furniture to freshen and unify disparate pieces. The fifth and final step for small-budget transformation is textile focused. Buy new pillows, recover or purchase new upholstery, and add a large sisal carpet to revitalize a tired room.

Alternatively, consider decorating over time, making an investment each year in an item or feature that brings you closer to your goal. Successful interior design differs from fashion in that it lasts longer—some rooms look great indefinitely and need only the occasional new bits and pieces (pillows, accessories) to revive good bones and keep them feeling fresh. The person who refuses to settle for something "not quite" will, in the long run, be happier with his or her environment than someone who is always buying the "almost" or "just okay." Although taking this tack requires patience and foresight, paradoxically the strategy of spending more money at first may save you some later.

When decorating your first home, a beach house or weekend place, or a transitional condo, you *can* put together something uncomplicated but still chic from big retailers, catalogs, and flea markets. Just know that the majority of it will not last, either literally (as in the sofa will give way—yes, fall apart!—in a few years) or figuratively (you'll get sick of the color scheme or trendy print on the drapery panels). If you go this route, stick with consistency and hold to a very tight color scheme. My recommendation for the furniture: go white. It is easy and elegant to have crisp white chairs, sofas, and tables against a gleaming dark floor or a boldly colored rug. Bring in a variety of colors through accents, throws, art, pillows, and china. When I mention this, people often reply, "But white? I can't. I need durable," and they end up with a convention of mushroom brown furniture. (Please, no!) Washable and bleachable white slipcovers made from denim, canvas, ticking, bleached duck (a heavy-weight upholstery cotton), linen, or other high-performance fabrics like faux leather and Ultrasuede would solve this problem.

Surface redecoration is not the only design project that you can successfully execute with a modest bank balance. You can also certainly be budget-minded when tackling seemingly major projects, like kitchen overhauls. Forget keeping up with the Joneses; if you do what everyone else does, you have to work really hard and spend a lot to differentiate yourself. But if you find a special niche, you can look great without killing yourself or your budget.

Case in point: The national average for a kitchen reno is more than $40,000, but I put together a young couple's kitchen for less than $20,000 from soup to nuts. The bones were basic and inexpensive. We started with lacquered white cabinets from IKEA and forwent the trendy professional stainless appliances that have become a little too popular in favor of sleek white-glass

ABOVE LEFT
Printed grass-cloth wallpaper provides undulating movement and height in a guest bedroom.

ABOVE, RIGHT AND OPPOSITE
Walls upholstered in individual panels of faux leather set vertically in a brick pattern, custom-made cabinetry, and a bedside table give every square inch of this tiny Manhattan bedroom function and interest.

Woodycrest Project for *Domino*

In the most challenging but rewarding and fun projects I've worked on in the past few years, my team and I decorated and furnished five two-bedroom apartments in a state-sponsored housing project in the Bronx for severely ill women and their children. This project was spearheaded by *Domino* magazine and conceived by a New York designer I greatly admire, Sara Bengur. Each designer was charged with creating rooms of great character and style but using only off-the-rack items—no custom work, no special orders, and no pieces costing more than a few hundred dollars. Several retailers, including Pier 1 Imports, JC Penney, and Pottery Barn opened their warehouses to us and, in an act of extreme generosity, gave us carte blanche to choose what we liked gratis to outfit the apartments.

I followed the "keep it simple" strategy and sought out commonly colored furnishings, textiles, and accessories across each of these store's product lines. In the living room, I used two coordinating textiles from my fabric line and a modified color palette of chocolate, acid green, and white from the corporate donated products. I matched the tiny rooms to one another as a way of cutting down on chaos and lending the space a highly controlled, customized design feel. For the mother's bedroom, calm, pale blue, cream, and brown were used; for the baby's room, turquoise, bright green, white, and acid yellow.

I relied on the trick of multiples to promote a cohesive, custom look and turn everyday objects into art. For example, in the living room I hung three identical mirrors over the sofa and used the same picture frames throughout the room. I also matched the lampshade fabric to the upholstery, a custom-looking detail that proved to be unifying and fun as well. Any furniture not in sync with the other finishes in the room (some whites were too white, others too cream), were primed and painted in the same Dove White Benjamin Moore color (also used on the ceiling and door trim). The nursery was decorated with a crib from JC Penney and made cheery by a bright quilt hung on the wall. (Art is what you frame.) I found large fabric butterflies and pinned them so that they fluttered up a corner of the room and continued their migration across the ceiling. One of the great advantages to decorating children's rooms is that they offer grown-ups a place to be fanciful and take risks. Putting together a kid's room is a bit like singing in the shower—you indulge fantasies, and if you make a mistake, no one begrudges you. Your taste in music and the room are both likely to change in a few years anyway.

A Shade of Invention

Making a traditional lampshade is an impressive and complicated art. But if you're looking for something offbeat, creative lighting and invented lampshades can be the right route to take. Old wicker and wire baskets, turned upside down, lend themselves to great hanging fixtures. Glass bell jars or cloches, used to cover delicate plants early in the growing season, also make beautiful chandeliers, as do old, oversized glass funnels (these should be taken to an experienced electrician to fit the wiring properly), or large, funnel-shaped metal sieves. Lampshades can also be fashioned out of baskets and buckets. For some easy and crafty-looking lamps, perfect for children's rooms and more whimsical settings, consider applying yarn, beads, gimp trim, paint, string, leather, feathers, or leaves to ready-made shades.

OPPOSITE

All three kitchens open into their living room areas, so the materials and finishes had to coordinate with the spaces they adjoin. As a note of interest, in the kitchen on the bottom, the entire wall of cabinetry can be wheeled away to reach the space's electrical panels.

LEFT AND BELOW

Green faux leather as wallpaper, white glass countertops, white glass–fronted appliances, white lacquer cabinets with Lucite accessories, and a Marmoleum floor make this kitchen inexpensive, clean, and colorful.

versions from Jenn-Air—great quality but less costly than the ubiquitous show-off stainless appliances, and most important, bright and spatially expanding. A sleek milk-colored composite glass countertop was inexpensive and practical. With a bright porcelain sink, we finished the gleaming and glossy kitchen.

Where I did splurge was on materials that were needed only in small doses for strong jolts of color. I wallpapered the very small room in a pungent lime faux leather from my line with Valtekz and added a Roman shade in a graphic, abstract floral pattern on the room's one window. These two features made an enormous impact because the rest of the kitchen was so flawlessly white. I chose custom Lucite hardware and shelves for their gleaming visual absence.

Design in the Fast Lane

In some situations, a house has to be put together quickly. With commitment, focus, decisiveness, and the willingness to shop from a combination of off-the-rack furniture suppliers, antiques stores, and auction houses, fast *is* feasible. London-based clients purchased a cozy weekend beach retreat in Amagansett, New York, which they planned on renting when not in residence. The deal closed at the end of March, and they had already lined up tenants for the first of July. That meant I had three months to order materials, paint, and furnish the home! Luckily my clients had bought well—the previous owners had good taste: architectural decisions were classic, and all the bones were good. The kitchen and bathrooms were in great condition—much to my relief considering redoing them in three months would have been impossible (at least on a reasonable budget).

Organization is mandatory within such a tight time frame. Planning, mulling over options, making decisions, shopping, and ordering take about a month, even when you have experience. Then it takes ten to twelve weeks of fabrication and shipping time to get everything delivered. Before the house is camera-ready, you need time to place, plump, fluff, stack, putter, and assess. Because I had worked with the couple on a previous apartment, they trusted my judgment and allowed me to make quick decisions on their behalf without the usual back-and-forth or a drawn-out approval process.

When speed is required, I go with simple floor plans and run through the checklist: a sofa, a pair of comfortable club chairs, a coffee table, side tables, a console table, and lighting. We ordered everything in one fell swoop using several of my favorite sources for accessible, reasonably priced, well-made furnishings. This is a good time to point out that there is a difference between the quality of furniture that comes from a mass-market home décor catalog and a dedicated furniture manufacturer (a few of my favorites being Baker, Century, Hickory Chair, and Laneventure, where I design my line). Because furniture making is the primary concern of these dedicated manufacturing companies, you can generally expect higher quality, and you can count on attention having been paid to details.

Room & Board, Bo Concept, West Elm, IKEA, Pier 1 Imports, Crate & Barrel, Pottery Barn, Restoration Hardware, Source Perrier, Wisteria, JC Penney, and Anthropologie all have fast turnaround and some great products. The ones that offer semicustom upholstery provide even a certain amount of flexibility and choice of fabrics as well as arm, leg, and back forms. Most items from these sources, even upholstered ones, will ship on a tight deadline (eight to twelve weeks—custom work takes longer). Just be sure never to buy a suite of seating from one place; mix it up so your room doesn't end up looking like a store or catalog display. And ask where the furniture is made and who produces it. You might get some informative answers. When they don't know or won't tell you, the lack of information should ring a few alarm bells.

We depended on many of the above sources to outfit the Amagansett house. Because it has a traditional style and is near the ocean, I chose a lot of white, blue, and sand-colored furniture, fabrics, and rugs. I went with strong but basic colors that are usually available in most

For speed, I based my paint colors on what I found in the bedding and rug marketplace. A stripe of orange in Restoration Hardware bed linens informed my wall paint selection in one bedroom, and their blue-gray sheet flanges inspired the custom wall color in another. Without a chance to check out the changing light in the new house, I used a designer trick and delved into my swatch book of high-end boutique mixed paints from Rollinson Hues. Trusting that the highly saturated pigments wouldn't shift much in varying lights, I was able to choose from the cold light of New York City for the misty bright light of the Hamptons.

product lines—chocolate brown, navy blue, bright green, and orange. By coordinating the accent colors in each room across the entire house and mixing a broad assortment of mass-manufactured furniture with eclectic vintage discoveries, I found both cohesion and character. I left some walls the original owner's choice of a pale buttery yellow. I painted others where I wanted to further a color choice we had made in rugs or bedding, in more dominant shades of blue-gray and persimmon orange.

As step one, I laid out a ½-inch floor plan of every room, drew seating arrangements, and used standard, ready-made sizes to orient the furniture (7-foot sofa, 36-inch-square chairs) and rugs (6 by 9, 8 by 10, and 9 by 12). I spent the bulk of the budget on long-term features like wallpaper, rugs, and curtains. We didn't have time for custom furniture or specially woven carpet: I had just enough time to order handmade curtains and a few custom-cut, -seamed and -bound larger-size sisal rugs. (Paying homage to the rule of the smaller the rug, the smaller the room appears, I made it a priority to get rugs that came within 18 inches of all walls. That exceeds the 12- or 13-foot max most retailers carry.)

The two "to the trade" fabrics that inspired the palettes for the family room and living room were used for curtains, which took a standard eight weeks to be made (the seamstresses were not working on them for that long; it is more a matter of getting on the maker's schedule . . . especially in the Hamptons, where everyone wants everything by July 1). The family room's design and color scheme started with a blue, green, and white medallion curtain fabric. I ordered a coordinating ikat-pattern blue rug and blue Laneventure Celerie chairs trimmed with white piping.

Instead of building or buying elaborate TV cabinets for the adjoining living/family rooms, I used console tables and flat screens on independent stands. We deliberately oriented the seating in both rooms around the fireplace because the TV was not going to be a priority at the beach house. Weekend occupants would more likely be outside, on the beach, or enjoying conversation around the fire on a chilly night.

Finally, I made several flea-market and junk-shop trips to the North Fork of Long Island and Dixie Highway in Florida for oddities and vintage items that would give the home an "acquired over time" and relaxed feel—its soul and its funk. Beall & Bell in Greenport, New York, proved a fantastic source of quirky, weathered, beachy antiques. Because Restoration Hardware offered sheets in numerous colors (a simple two-stripe pattern on a clean white) and prefabricated curtains and sheers in corresponding colors of Belgian linen, we chose them for guestroom bed linens and ready-made curtains.

By July 1 the house was put together and comfortable, though I have continued to work with the clients to fill in a few blanks or add pieces. The house is still waiting for the character and layers of personality its owners will bring to it over the years as they spend more of their time there and find art and antiques that are meaningful. Like all houses, this one will continue to evolve and, long after my work is done, become seasoned and beloved as it should.

With commitment, focus, decisiveness, and the willingness to shop from a combination of off-the-rack furniture suppliers, antiques stores, and auction houses, fast is feasible.

Lighting

The standard-issue lighting that comes with most apartments and spec houses is inadequate or just plain awful (not enough, too harsh, or flat). A good lighting plan must be developed. Bad lighting, either too much (the lab-rat phenomenon) or too little (low-budget horror movie), is physically exhausting on the eyes, depressing for the spirit, and miserable for our egos. Nothing signals the end of a cocktail or dinner party like a trip to a poorly lit powder room. With huge shadows under my eyes and a caught-in-the-headlights, soon-to-be-roadkill blanched-skin look, I'm suddenly five minutes from "Thank you and good night" so I can run for my bed.

We want to feel lovely, whether we're brushing our teeth, trying on an outfit, chatting with a friend on the sofa, or sitting at our dining table. Warm glowing lights, appropriate task lighting, and the ability to manipulate mood and functionality make the experience of a space uplifting or calming. Whether you love to entertain or you're a loner, remember that lighting is an essential element of comfort, mood, and, often, self-esteem. The best lighting combines both science and art—successful plans help us to read and play and cook and bathe but also make us look better and feel festive, romantic, or ready to conquer the world.

Plenty of home-improvement books adequately describe the technical aspects of lighting, but I will share a few lighting-design tricks of the trade and some basic advice. First, one overhead light centered in the ceiling is simply not enough to create ambiance, warmth, or even enough brightness to sort the mail or wrangle a bag into the vacuum cleaner. More important, it's not becoming for your complexion: without the support of sidelights and lamps, a single overhead lamp will cast deep shadows under the eyes and nose, making everyone in the room look tired and sallow. This direct beam of light is an ugly thing; avoid the "flashlight problem" by having a multiplicity of both bright (but controllable) and subtle light sources at different levels around a room: recessed and directional, hanging fixtures, sconces, up lights in plants, table and floor lamps, natural light, and firelight (candles, oil lamps, or hearth).

Practical Matters

General lighting provides even, overall brightness. It is essential that you have this basic in place everywhere, along with the ability to control groups of lights with switches, and dimmers that can change brightness levels (dimmers should really be installed on all lighting fixtures in your house, if possible, including lamps. If not, buy three-way bulbs). Recessed lighting, the most efficient form of general overall illumination, provides an even, all-over glow. On the downside, the installation requires a 4- to 5-inch loss of ceiling height where the "high hats" are installed, so they can be flush with the ceiling. In some rooms the sacrifice is worthwhile. If your ceilings are more than 8½ feet high, the loss of ceiling height is barely perceptible. Recessed lighting just disappears—you notice the illumination, not the fixture. The evenly distributed light makes the room feel larger. If possible, select recessed lights that swivel so you can direct one or more toward art, wash a wall in brightness, or highlight a seating arrangement, when desired.

OPPOSITE
This guest bathroom in a Florida house is thematically charged, with all the design elements relating to shells and bamboo. The shell-encrusted chandelier and bamboo molding make the greatest statement.

Bright Ideas

Subtly tinted bulbs (pink, peach) in lamps add a soft glow to a room. Three-way bulbs take the place of dimmers in table lamps. Some bulbs (such as the Varilus T10 in a 25-watt version) make colors vivid and are my favorite for picture lights.

Track lighting is a similar option but comes at greater cost—clutter in one of the few places we've really come to expect minimalism, your broad expanse of ceiling. Even modern versions look like dangling braces or appear commercial; think jewelry-store and fast-food counters. Whichever kind of fixture you use, don't forget to place groups of lights on separate switches so you have the flexibility to light all or some.

Hanging fixtures are different, and there's no need to limit them to formal rooms. Consider one for the master bedroom and bathroom or anywhere a light centered in the room won't make the furniture plan feel off-kilter. Freeing the hanging fixture from the responsibility of providing all the light in a room allows you to use it for decorative impact. A flush-mounted fixture is rarely as visually effective as a hanging chandelier or pendant, so reserve them for use only in areas of very low ceiling height or in areas that can't take the centering described above. Even if you have low ceilings, you can still choose a semiflush fixture, which extends slightly down from the ceiling and affords the feeling of a hanging fixture without taking up valuable headroom.

I'm often asked if a fail-safe formula exists to determine the hanging length of a chandelier above a table. I use the following guideline and then eyeball it: hang the fixture so the bottom is 31 inches above the table. People mistakenly hang chandeliers more often too high than too low. When in doubt, drop it a touch to avoid that institutional feel.

There are rarely enough electrical outlets in pre-1970 houses. So, if you are renovating an older house or building, make every effort to add necessary outlets to your rooms, but do so in your base moldings if you can. Cords are ugly and no one wants to see them skulking around. I've noticed that the owners of new buildings get a little overzealous with outlets, placing them every 4 to 5 feet at a height of about 14 inches above the baseboards. It is easy to cap the ones you won't use in order to keep them from interrupting your wall surface unnecessarily.

Easily reachable power sources offer tremendous flexibility in placing lamps and helping conceal wires but they should be clustered behind headboards, armoires, and chests. You can also have outlets in the floor, which is especially helpful when a couch is "floating" in the middle of a room backed by a console table that can hold reading lamps. One of the reasons I like putting sisal rugs on the floor is that you can easily cut them to run an electric cord through and under to the closest outlet.

Short of having new floor outlets installed, the decorator's trick is to tape the cord on the floor and run it all the way to the outlet (replace short lamp wire with long—you can buy it by the yard at any hardware store), then lay a carpet pad over it and cut the pad on either side of the cord so you can remove that piece and the cord is flush with the pad. The rug goes on top and no one's the wiser. In desperate situations I also run cords behind the bottom of curtains and staple them to baseboards. Paint the cord the same color as the molding and it really disappears. Plants also provide wonderful camouflage on either side or under a console table and

OPPOSITE

It's exciting to find an antique in a rare color that can bring a room together. Here, a vintage red wood bobble-painted chandelier does the trick.

BELOW

In new construction, an antique lighting fixture adds character that a new fixture would lack.

on top of cords to hide them . . . or put a large basket or an ottoman or two under tables to hide wires.

If you have a cabinet pressed against a wall, plug all your lights and other equipment into flat-backed extension cords and run them behind the cabinet. If you have equipment inside the cabinet that requires electricity, drill a single hole in the back of the cabinet and connect an internally housed surge protector to the flat-backed cord. This little extension cord means you don't have to leave 2 inches between your cabinet and the wall as you would with the thicker-headed traditional extension cords.

For bathrooms and kitchens, the lighting must be flexible, with a range from operating-room bright for certain tasks to mellow and ambient for guests and late-night baths. It is most important for the bathroom to have varying levels of light so that self-examination doesn't become cruel. Wall sconces should go on either side of the bathroom mirror. A chandelier set on a dimmer offers soft, soothing light when makeup application isn't the goal. If there is room, in addition to hanging overhead fixtures, I add a small lamp to a table or a vanity to create a warm, all-over lighting story. In kitchens, undercabinet halogen puck lighting provides excellent brightness with the added benefit of being discreet.

Wall Fixtures

Sconces are lighting jewelry because they have such a strong decorative effect in a room. They bring in light at midlevel, which evens out the overhead lighting. When light comes only from above, any objects or furniture not bathed in it look forlorn and belittled. Wall sconces also bring brightness to the sides and corners of rooms, by fireplaces or large mirrors. Soft light washes around the room, making it appear much bigger because illumination warms and highlights the farthest peripheries.

Lighting need not be expensive to be glamorous. Event the grittiest, down-at-the-heels skyline looks like a bed of jewels when the lights come on at night. If you cannot afford or find the exact sconces you want right away, buy something inexpensive and have the wiring done so that when the ones you're looking for appear, it's easy enough to install them. Don't let fear of expensive construction and electrical jobs stop you from adding wall sconces to your house. Instead, look for those that come with cord covers built in; they are easy to install into an existing plug.

As for placement, there is no hard and fast rule. A too-common mistake, which I've also pointed out as prevalent with chandeliers and artwork, is installing sconces too high. Most people install them 6 to 7 feet above the floor, but I prefer to place sconces at 61 to 68 inches (closer to eye level).

I always hardwire picture and bookcase lights into the walls once I know where the artwork and shelves are going. They serve a double purpose: ostensibly used to highlight a painting, photograph, or set of books, they also work as ambient lights for entertaining (and even as night-lights). For parties, I often leave on a light or two in my bookcase and then fill the living room with candlelight only.

ABOVE
Frond-like beams of illumination radiate outward from these vintage lights, adding drama to an otherwise simple hallway.

OPPOSITE
A pair of hand-blown, copper-toned, mirrored, gourd-like hanging fixtures leave the room's surface area uncluttered and offer an unusual alternative to table lamps or wall sconces.

A Little Night Magic: In Praise of Dappling

My mother, Mimi McMakin, taught me the magic of shadow casting. She has always sought out lighting that throws distinctive shadows, going so far as to design a table with this in mind. It is glass-topped with a base of perforated metal shaped like a giant pineapple. In the center of the pineapple there is space for an up light or a candle, which shines through the cutouts in diffused and unexpected dappled patterns. The same thing happens when you place an up light beneath a potted palm or citrus tree—light coming up through the leaves spreads a striking pattern on the wall and ceiling. Perforated chandeliers or lampshades perform a similar trick.

Lamps

I love table lamps, if only for the sheer variety of style and their versatility. I'm partial to pairs of lamps placed on either side of a sofa, or on a console behind a sofa. A good way to use an oddball lamp that does not have a matching sister is to place it atop a chest of drawers. Caution: You'll want to avoid having more than two pairs of similarly scaled lamps at the same height in one room unless you differentiate them with shades of distinct shapes and styles. Otherwise it's like having four sisters in the same room, all wearing the same hat. Look for standing lamps, perhaps a pharmacy lamp or one with a painted metal shade as a special reading light behind a comfortable chair, candlestick lamps for inside bookcases or on a bureau, or a bouillotte lamp (a traditional lamp with candlesticks surrounding one main light source, usually with a metal or tole shade). Lastly, put some up lights beneath your trees and nestled at their base. The effect is beautiful at little cost.

As for lampshades, while they should be sympathetic to the style of the lamp, they should not be imprisoned by its period or style. For example, if you have a little-old-lady lamp and a modern lamp, I'd try the same modern shade on both or do different shades, each suited to its base, but in the same fabric. In any case, no bright white and no straight cylinders. Some narrowing at the top of a shade, even if it is subtle, is proportionally more pleasing. Cream or natural-tone

ABOVE AND OPPOSITE, ABOVE
Delicate blown-glass and shell light fixtures are the jewelry in this child-filled Manhattan apartment. The ceiling is a great canvas for fragile and precious objects if their destruction is guaranteed elsewhere!

OPPOSITE, BELOW
Vintage shipyard lights add authenticity to a newly installed tin ceiling.

parchment shades are the most relaxed and versatile, while stark white paper shades always seem brazen and unfinished in a room that does not use stark white as an accent.

One or two black shades add gravitas to a room; so don't be afraid of this strong statement. Other opaque shades may come lined with gold or silver to send light up and down so the light does not shine in your eyes when the lamp is resting on a table. Soft pastel-colored silk shades lend their pale tint to almost imperceptibly diffuse light so that it emanates in all directions. Occasionally in rooms dominated by one or two colors, a punch of color in the form of a lamp-shade adds some pop.

As for length and scale, be sure the shade you choose is just long enough to cover up the switch but not so long that it covers the top of the neck of the lamp: like a man in pants that are too short, a lamp looks gangly this way. In general, shades should be about one-third of the overall height of your lamp, no matter the size of your room. If you are struggling with a decision about shade shape, look to the lamp base and bring the lamp with you when shopping. Try a few on just as you would clothes. The subtlety of a perfect fit is something that's easier to see when you can look at it as an editor or stylist.

In small rooms, coordinate all the material lampshades even if you have both antique lamps and very modern ones. The shades do not have to match the lamp styles but you can unify different lamp forms in the room by using shades of related color or tone but not necessarily exact style. (Unifying all lamps is not as important in a large room, where lamps do not risk looking like overused exclamation points.)

Firelight

Candles are the least expensive, easiest form of versatile lighting in a room. Natural beeswax candles are lovely because they burn slowly and evenly, never drip, and have a heavenly subtle perfume, though they're not scented. Even while unlit, they are the prettiest, so they always rest in any of the unelectrified chandeliers or wall sconces I hang. I don't particularly like colored candles unless they are thematically relevant to a party, but I do love a scented candle in the entryway, powder room, or bedroom (though not in the dining room, where the scent interferes with the food). Or I store them, with favorite scented soaps, in my lingerie drawer and linen cabinet, wrapped in tissue, so that my clothing and sheets pick up their scent.

Votives are the best and cheapest way to create a party mood. Go with a single style and have lots of them around a room. Tea lights encircled in silver foil are certainly easier to clean with their metal bases, but they look a bit junky en masse, so I opt for placing 2-inch-tall votives in glass holders and just deal with the digging and scraping at the wax when I need to clean the glasses. I am also partial to oil lamps—a nice change from votives. They don't put out quite as much heat as candles do, don't drip, and don't usually have any scent. Remember that candles and oil lamps placed in front of mirrors add twice the sparkle. Also keep in mind that lit candles should never be left unattended, and beware children and pets in a room with candlelight.

LEFT
Remember, curtains don't always have to fall straight to the floor. A shaped edge can cut a new architectural line into the incoming light from a window. This curtain adds a sweeping gesture to an otherwise box-like room.

Controlling Natural Light

The natural glow of a spring day or the long amber light of an early-evening fall sunset can be warm and flattering, but the glare and heat of uncontrolled natural light can overwhelm us. That is why the management of windows is a key part of the lighting design. Curtains and sheers are adaptable. They cut down on bright sun, diffuse visibility to allow for privacy, and can provide total darkness for sleeping and watching movies. I have all but given up on using blackout curtains because, even when made beautifully in the traditional fashion with bump, blackout, and interlining, the bulk of the fabrics makes the curtains hard to close. The synthetic backing of inferior blackout curtains is lighter but doesn't drape as well. Either way, light will still seep out beneath the rings if you don't have a valance. The exception to these two problems is found in instances in which traverse rods and electrified tracks that run by remote control can be installed, or when windows are very small.

For complete light elimination, I usually turn to honeycomb shades, wooden blinds, or a concealed roller shade. No one wants to see the blackout element (it often looks like a blank tarp), so I put a sheer or natural fiber shade in front to disguise these purely functional contraptions. The addition of curtain panels on either side creates a vertical as well as a blanketed, layered look. If you don't want a lot of material, you can still go with the inexpensive blackout shade and then put a

sheer Roman shade or lightly perforated sheers in front of it. Always buy the highest-grade mechanism available. Durability is as much an issue as ease of use because groggy, lazy people will leave them down all day or up at night rather than wrestle with an ineffective shade pull.

In a room that gets very strong sun, use a sheer as a base, with heavier curtains on a double rod so that both fabric panels can be used to control the light. My inclination is to mix a natural element in as well, in the form of bamboo, grass cloth, or wooden-matchstick blinds under the sheers. These materials also contribute a strong horizontal to contrast with the long, vertical fabric. Pay attention to trims on the drapes, as they provide an easy way to pump up the impact or subtly reference the rest of your overall scheme. Trims are easy because they can be hand sewn or applied with fabric glue if you can manage to hold a straight line with pins down the end of your curtain. (This is one of the few truly simple DIY tricks I haven't botched yet!)

And curtains should touch or "kiss" the floor by about $\frac{1}{2}$ to 2 inches for more drama. Except in boats, bistros, and country cottages, I have never used half-height curtains. You'll also want the treatment to look abundant in width. Fabric that stretches two and a half times the width of the window is preferable, but you can get away with a one-and-a-half width if budget is an issue.

Small Is Beautiful

Many people these days are downsizing from big suburban spreads to more earth-friendly and manageable small homes (1,500 square feet or less, in many cases). And many urban dwellers pack cooking, eating, entertaining, relaxing, working, and sleeping into 750 square feet (or less!). Small does not have to equal desperate or dreary. More and more manufacturers are realizing that not everyone lives or wants to live big, and are making stylish furniture and appliances sized for more modest spaces. That's a key component to designing a small space since the single most important way to make an undersized room feel bigger is to furnish it with appropriately scaled furniture and other features. Do not, under any circumstances, buy one of those "chair and a half" monsters with the thought that more chair equals more seating. It doesn't. Any upholstered seating with exceptionally wide arms or a thick back takes up too much of your room with nonfunctional features. As I've suggested, focus instead on the interior depth and width to ensure that most of a piece's construction is actually for sitting.

Several other tricks can be used to make a small room seem larger and more impressive. The best decorating help for your space is often to subtract from it. Aside from not taking up all the space with oversized furnishings, your aim is to cut down on visual chaos. Keep it simple. Stick with a basic palette of three colors, keep accessories bold in form and tone, but to a minimum in quantity for maximum impact. Buy the longest sofa you can (you can go down to about 72 inches before a sofa feels tiny), but one with narrow arms, and cover it in a solid or big bold print—no fussy minipatterns. A small club chair is an ideal accompaniment, but short of that even a wooden armchair with an upholstered seat is a plus. One pair is nicer, if you have room. If a coffee table is off limits because of space, consider multiple matching stools or small ottomans in durable fabrics that can be easily configured into side tables, a cocktail table, or extra seating.

In addition to helping with light issues, mirrors also help overcome space challenges. In small dressing rooms or bathrooms, mirror all the doors and walls to create the illusion of greater space. Frame an almost-floor-to-ceiling mirror and lean it on a wall in any room of the house to double the perceived area. Open up a living room/dining room by installing mirror panes in French doors that remain closed most of the time.

Another decorator's space-enlarging trick, no matter the size of your windows, is to dress them by putting the shade high above its frame so the window looks as if it extends nearly up to the ceiling. Then, add curtain side panels that don't cover the window but flank it at least a foot beyond either side of the frame.

If you plan to use a rug, use the biggest one you can so it nearly covers the entire floor. As I've said, a small rug in the center of a small room diminishes the perception of square footage.

When it comes to color and pattern in diminutive spaces, go for it. The smaller the room, the more saturated the color and the more dramatic its patterns should be. This isn't playing with fire as much as it sounds. A clutter of color or texture is very different from the clutter of objects. You can keep the palette tight or limited to two or three colors, as I have said, but

Best Cabinetry Ideas for Small Spaces

- Surround windows with bookcases to create a library setting and fill the areas below the bottom sill with cushions to the same depth as the casing around them. This makes the window a centerpiece, and provides an area for a comfy curl up and an eye-refreshing spot of upholstery in all the wood. Built in drawers and shelves under the window seat can be used for extra storage.
- When building fitted wall shelves, be sure to have deeper lower cabinets made. On the shelf of extra depth, you can place art on an easel, large illustrated books, a tray, or a bar of buffet items—and they won't need to take up precious space on a coffee table.
- In a small kitchen, paint all the cabinetry white and cover the floor (or paint it if it is wood) with a dark, bold color. Add splashes of bright fabric for contrast but unity.

LEFT
Mirroring on shoe-cabinet doors makes this small walk-in closet feel larger. All of the closed drawers either have faux shagreen facing or are left as glass, offering jewel-box detail and easy viewing.

OPPOSITE
A sink runs wall to wall, filling the niche of this powder room. Wall-mounted fixtures save on counter depth. Large-scale patterned wallpaper lends this tiny space significance.

Small-Space Saviors

A magnetic knife wall rack

Ottomans with built-in storage

A hall or bedroom closet refitted as your office

Big baskets—they help you clean up clutter fast

A tall bed—or one on risers—for instant extra
   storage beneath

Bookshelves built around and on top of doorways

Mirrored walls or furniture

OPPOSITE
*Mirroring a whole wall
doubles the perception of
space and multiples your
windows.*

RIGHT
*Papering the ceiling in a
small space like this
bathroom makes a treasure
of a tiny room. Vertical
stripes draw the eye
upward.*

BELOW
*The mirrored backsplash
behind a bar gives the
illusion of depth and
fresh air.*

OPPOSITE
*Vertical stripes and low
horizontal furniture add
height to the extremely low
ceiling in the attic of a
suburban house, above. In a
room with no moldings,
below, we upholstered the
walls and the front of the
plain closet doors with a
mellow zebra-printed linen.
Using the same fabric for
curtains expands the walls.
The canopied daybed
provides its own room within
a room, and internal
architecture. Even the
scalloped table hides nesting
bookcases to maximize space.*

BELOW
*Storage may be a necessity,
but often I don't want to call
attention to a utility space
and will paper right over it.*

they should make a statement. After all, you have less wall space and surface area for accessories. Making a major declaration with bold fabrics and strong colors can distract from square-footage limitations. Don't restrict yourself to the conventional light colors or small prints. Use wallpaper in a large-scale pattern, or upholster the walls in a similarly dramatic fabric. On occasion, I use the same pattern on the walls as on the upholstery; having less contrast between the furniture and the walls seems to make you perceive the space as larger. It's a deceptively simple play for inches that really works.

Awkward Architecture

In general, you can go in two opposite directions with architecturally challenging features: finesse them so they are far less noticeable or play them up so they are conspicuous in a deliberate way. Resorting to wholesale reconstruction has to happen less frequently than you think. Perfect example: a show-house living room I designed in the Hamptons had French doors and beautiful windows, but the fireplace was off center from the windows, a common problem in many homes with large living areas or great rooms. Moving the doors or firebox was not in the parameters of the job, and would have been too expensive and impractical. We could have oriented the seating arrangement toward the French doors or the windows but this would have actually made the fireplace appear even more off center, since it was the first thing you saw when you entered the room.

The fireplace remained the focal point, but the windows became the center point of the room. I visually "moved" the hearth forward into the room by placing two chairs in front of it to function as an independent seating arrangement. I then centered the sofa between the two windows and pulled its accompanying wing chairs toward the fireplace seating area by placing a console behind them to bump them out into the room. In general, symmetrical arrangements force asymmetrical architectural features into alignment. The larger or more cavernous the room, the more necessary symmetry is because it helps knit the room together.

Uneven or varied ceiling heights in the same room are also an issue in many homes. For example, houses built in the pre-Victorian and Colonial eras, and even many built in the 1950s and 1960s, commonly have very low ceilings—sometimes as low as 7 or 8 feet (as opposed to today's heights of 9 or 10 feet). New homes often feature great rooms with very high "vaulted" ceiling areas next to conventional flat, low ceilings. Many modern and contemporary apartments and lofts have two different ceiling heights in the same open space because ductwork or other mechanical or electrical complications require the ceiling to be "built out" to accommodate wiring or pipes.

In these situations I usually paint the ceilings in a flat finish of a slightly lighter color than the walls and trim to make them appear taller and unified. When and where I can, I avoid flat white ceilings. The responsibility to select a color shouldn't be forgotten on this "fifth wall." People sometimes become hung up on selecting a color on a ceiling that travels between several rooms uninterrupted. But the walls of those rooms, if they open into one another, probably share a similar base color of cream (warm colors) or white (cool colors). Look to replicate that color on the ceiling of each room and trim instead of painting it copy-paper white.

In the instance of low ceilings or those complicated with dropped areas and beams, I often wallpaper or paint the lower beams the same color as the wall. Deciding which beams to paint or paper, as a continuation of the wall or ceiling, is the tricky part. If there is a consistent minority of ceiling height that's significantly higher than the beam height, I try to accent the higher bits as much as I can and take credit for that as the "true" ceiling height. Accentuating those scraps of ceilings with paper or grass cloth and visually obscuring or distracting from the beams with plain paint achieves this trick.

You can define the ceiling surface by faux painting it, papering it, adding a special treatment to the ceiling, or applying a distinctive molding between the beams and ceiling. In my apartment (a converted hotel), the ceiling in the living room presented just this problem with a patchwork of ductwork and beams. To accentuate the highest area, the flats of the ceiling, and not the lower hanging beams, I applied grass-cloth wallpaper to the beams and applied bamboo trim between them and what I was going to acknowledge as ceiling. I also used grass cloth to cover the columns in the space, adding to a feeling of continuity and attempting to visually define anything I didn't like as mere background.

Favorite Fixes for Miscellaneous Architectural Issues

Dark rooms. To improve light in a naturally dark room, move its entryway door so that it is positioned across from a lighter room's window, if possible. That way you can borrow light and create perceived access to the other window. Pocket or French doors are best in this situation. If it is not possible to move the door, add a mirror to the wall facing a window to cheat more light into the space.

Dull doors. If doors on closets, unused exits, and passageways look plain, cover them with the wall treatment you have used to achieve one continuous sweep. Or, hang art on the backs of doors, especially one that you envision treating as a wall. If the adjoining walls are covered in molding, apply it to the doors, too, so that they blend in.

Worrisome walls. If you have poor-quality walls, use a wallpaper liner and heavy-duty paper such as grass cloth or paint and apply latticework over a contrasting color.

Window envy. Not enough windows? Place oversize paintings, photographs, and mirrors or mirrored furniture where you'd like windows to be and decorate around them as though they were really openings—place sconces on either side, or orient seating toward them so you can enjoy "the view." These pieces will create an artificial sense of scale, balance, and breathing-room vistas that real windows would offer.

Instant Architecture

I still think one of the most environmentally friendly moves you can make is to recycle old elements. Try to revive, reuse, scavenge, or buy antique or vintage. You can buy entire paneled walls, wainscoting, old fireplaces and mantels, and spectacular windows and doors from old houses and install them in your room, adding character where it may not exist. Many salvage companies and large auction houses offer these relics of artistry, craftsmanship, and history, rescued from old houses that are set for demolition. Check the yellow pages or online for "salvage companies" or "antique architecture." Depending on the age, detail, and condition of the salvaged piece, its price can either be similar to purchasing simple lumberyard stock or less-than-custom fabrication depending on the source you buy it from.

For vertical emphasis and to create interest and symmetry on walls, apply picture frame molding, from either new or salvaged stock. If your budget is supertight, consider painting on molding—sometimes the faux versions are more interesting and beautiful than the real thing.

OPPOSITE

If space, taste, or mechanical reality such as an air-conditioning vent makes molding application complicated, faux-painted moldings are often a practical and interesting alternative.

BELOW LEFT

Opening a double-sided wine cabinet between the kitchen and living room places an unexpected "window" and light source in two rooms. See page 44 for the opposite side.

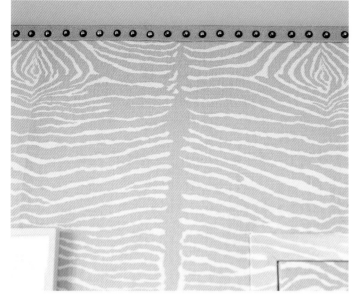

OPPOSITE
Husband and wife disagreed about the importance of speakers. We obscured their view from inside the bed with a canopy and pelmet.

ABOVE LEFT
A jute tape trim applied with large brass nail heads takes the place of crown molding in this room, and faux painting covers an unimpressive door surround and allows the illusion of continued wall upholstery despite the presence of doors.

ABOVE RIGHT
Only one element of the extremely decorative pitched ceiling is actually three-dimensional. The rest is painted—a brilliant Colfax & Fowler trick.

Some less-than-appealing aspects of a room are best dealt with by disguising them—call it realistic reconfiguration. In a prewar Park Avenue three-bedroom, two-and-a-half-bath apartment, some investigatory demolition in the master closet and guest room closet revealed that each held a hidden window. Though they both looked out on a sooty air shaft, they were windows nonetheless—precious commodities in New York City. Because the illusion of egress and fresh air was all we could ask of these windows, I suspended a softly gathered sheer inside mount Roman shade entirely over the window and then hung a large trifold mirror in front of that. This trick suggested a pleasant window. The reflection from the pair of large windows across the bedroom amplified and bounced the single source of natural light around both rooms.

Modern (In)Conveniences

Many of the mechanical necessities of modern life have presented obstacles to good design. Not so long ago the seven-shelf stereo unit, skyscraper-tall CD towers, and mammoth computer setups created the need for something called a media room—a repository for black metal boxes, thick tangles of cables and wires, melamine shelves, and black leather recliners, complete with built-in cup holders. I'm no Luddite, it's just that I want to *use,* not subordinate myself to, technology. That's why, as our techie items get progressively more petite, it becomes easier to minimize the design impact of technology. I am willing to pay up to go down in size, or invest in cabinets or other tricks to house electronics with discretion. The trade-off of the cost of expensive minitechnology versus the cost per square foot you lose with large technology in your house or apartment might surprise you if you do the math.

BlackBerries, iPods, flat-screen TVs, and laptops can virtually disappear when properly placed. For example (Steve Jobs deserves a kiss for this!), when the iPod is plugged into a small but powerful docking-station or perched discreetly on a bookshelf speaker system, you can consider throwing out the receiver, the dedicated tape deck, or bulky CD player. That little gadget alone took three bulky components out of the game. If you are a sound connoisseur and must have special (read: large) or particularly (read: overtly) placed speakers, try to keep them in the ceiling, nestled flush in soffits, or stored neatly on bookshelves. Whether dangling from above or standing alone, exposed speakers are not ideal, but you can paint or purchase them in the same color as the wall or ceiling so they are a bit less conspicuous.

Plug Away

When building new, renovating, or rebuilding, have your electrician hide outlets in drawers and inside cabinets, especially in bathrooms (for hair dryers and electric shavers), kitchens, and bedrooms.

Historically, the fireplace or hearth was central to a room's activity. In many instances of modern life, TV has taken this role. As such, the television should be opposite comfortable seating (the sofa in a living room, or the bed or a love seat in a bedroom). But arranging around lifestyle shouldn't mean good looks go out the window. A TV hulking dominantly over any room is almost always an eyesore.

Flat screens have presented a major solution for TV bulk, but I would still do my best to hide them. It's now possible to close them in a shallow cabinet or antique armoire (which used to be notoriously skimpy for the depth of old-fashioned sets). If the technology must remain out in the open, you can make it less obtrusive by obscuring it in a bookshelf; setting it in a peripheral wall with a swing arm bracket so it can be angled to multiple viewpoints; surrounding it with distracting art; or flanking it with tall elements. Is the TV used daily or occasionally? If infrequently, hide it under a skirted table and pull it out whenever necessary. If you must place the TV above a fireplace or a console table, come up with ways to hide it when it's not in use. For instance, I like to build out a wall 4 or 5 inches so the flat screen is truly flush with the wall but attached to a pivot mechanism that allows you to pull it out and turn it in any direction. Then, hang art over it. Two picture hooks are all you need for this trick: one goes right above the set to hang the picture so it covers the screen, and the other goes higher, to move the art to when you want to watch TV (be sure to paint the hooks the same color as the wall, so they disappear).

Or, as you may have already done, just give in to the brazen TV that has, in many ways, come to represent the modern-day hearth. Even if you're going with the "it's there; I'm not going to kill myself trying to hide it" approach, flat screens have depth that ideally can be planned for, though you will still need to find a place to hide the cable box and DVD player until technology makes these smaller too.

OPPOSITE
A TV placed between two windows disappears entirely when the metal bookshelf on a gliding track rolls in front.

Design Innovations

Today there is a tremendous amount of design technology that many people forget about or aren't aware of, such as remote-controlled items from window shades and curtains to heating and cooling systems, even patio awnings. It is now possible to draw your shades or change the temperature in your bedroom from your BlackBerry. Many new, man-made, "green" or ecologically sustainable materials and textiles offer intriguing design possibilities and increased durability—paving the way for previously unheard-of design choices such as pale-colored carpets and linenlike upholstery for a mother of three.

OPPOSITE
In this glass-fronted cabinet there was no absolute way to hide a TV, so we obscured it within an arrangement of objects.

RIGHT
When the easy solution of pocket doors or cabinet doors that open out are not an option, remember you can still go up with a sliding shelf.

BELOW
The least technical of all TV disguises: find and hang appropriately scaled art, which can be moved to an adjoining wall when the television is in use.

Tiny Technology

Eliminate the big computer setup and opt for a laptop at home if possible. Most of us really do not need more power than these trim little electronic notebooks offer. If you do, consider a fully separate office space to shut out the nagging stress that symbols of "connectedness" can create. Even if the computer is turned off, seeing it still reminds me of what I need to do when I turn it on. A laptop allows any room in your house to be a comfortable, quiet spot—releasing the tether to one chair or one bulky desk in the den. Besides, it's nice to be able to get up and move around to work where the light is best, the seat most appealing, and the spot of solitude beckons.

RIGHT
Vine-covered wallpaper crawls up the walls to the ceiling and covers it save for the center, which is adorned with an aged mirror that reflects an antique rock crystal chandelier. The treatment creates a soaring and interesting (one-of-a-kind) ceiling.

In the kitchen, I like the idea of refrigerators and dishwasher "drawers," oven doors that open to the side instead of down (for safer and easier access to hot food), and panels that can be replaced on appliances so that they literally blend in with the woodwork. Being partial to white or painted-wood kitchens, I find custom-facing appliances to match cabinetry to be a great advantage.

Bathroom inventions—shower "tiles" that sit flush with the wall and ceiling to create an all-over spray; mood lighting built into soaking tubs, which by the way can be as big as swimming pools if you have the space—continue to amaze. I am conflicted about modern toilets. Excellent service records and the environmental considerations of lower water usage have begun to sway me from my earlier diehard loyalty to the vintage or retro-styled porcelain ones. But the designs of the modern toilets have not captured my heart quite yet . . . I always feel as if I am in a commercial setting when I see the aggressive speedboat style of some of the plastic versions. Since a bathroom is to be functional by its very nature, jewelry-like elements and curvaceous porcelain are much more appealing to me, and an old-fashioned toilet, tub, or sink is one of the most likely ways to indulge those whims.

Finally, radiant-heat floors have transformed the bathroom experience. Deliciously warm underfoot, especially if you live in a cold climate, they take away that ripped-from-the-womb feeling when you step out of the shower or bath. No matter where you live, it's very nice to have a bit of coddling before you face the harsh, cold realities of the real world.

Modern life runs at lightning speed, and the biggest design dilemma of all might be to figure out how to find the time to enjoy the space you've created. I certainly don't always juggle everything successfully in my life—I hear the constant crash of balls dropping as I run out the door to the next appointment. But I try never to forget that my family's and my experience of our home is one of the most important things in life. There's nothing better than taking a long soak in my tub, or curling up on the sofa with my husband, son, and dog and just relaxing. Design problems become minimal when you are just having a good time. Perhaps the ultimate design solution, then, is to develop a big appetite for fun.

Art Meets Commerce

Necessary "no-tech" conveniences can pose design issues in the bathroom and kitchen. I say go with what you've *got* to have and "love your kit." Since we are surrounded by product, we may as well turn it into art. When you see something you need that is charmingly packaged, purchase in multiples. Think of visible consumption items as part of your permanent and evolving environment. Some people who will pay an extra $1,500 for a name-brand refrigerator balk at paying an extra 50¢ for the prettier toothpaste tube. Stacks or bowls full of everyday objects make a powerful statement. A pyramid of tissue rolls in a glass-fronted cabinet is the perfect crossroad of attractive storage and interactive sculpture. A row of beautiful canned goods or gorgeous glass water bottles looks charming on an open kitchen shelf.

Personal-product choices are highly individual but I love Marvis toothpaste (both the packaging and its taste), so I pile tubes of it in a large glass container that sits on a counter in my bathroom. I even go so far as to buy makeup or body wash as much for its packaging as I do for its scent and efficacy. After lots of searching and sampling, I've become devoted to Jo Malone and Nars products—each makes my favorite scents and makeup and puts them in packaging that is tailor-made for a black-and-white bathroom scheme.

When the products I need aren't packaged attractively, I transfer them to clear glass bottles or jars. Take book jackets with garish colors. I remove them, and allow the less-obtrusive binding color to take a starring role, or I cover the book with a simple white or brown kraft-paper cover. This may seem excessive, but it's really no different than camouflaging the hallway fuse box with artwork or paint.

Remember, if your stroller is going to spend a percentage of every day in your entry hall or living room, buy a color that coordinates.

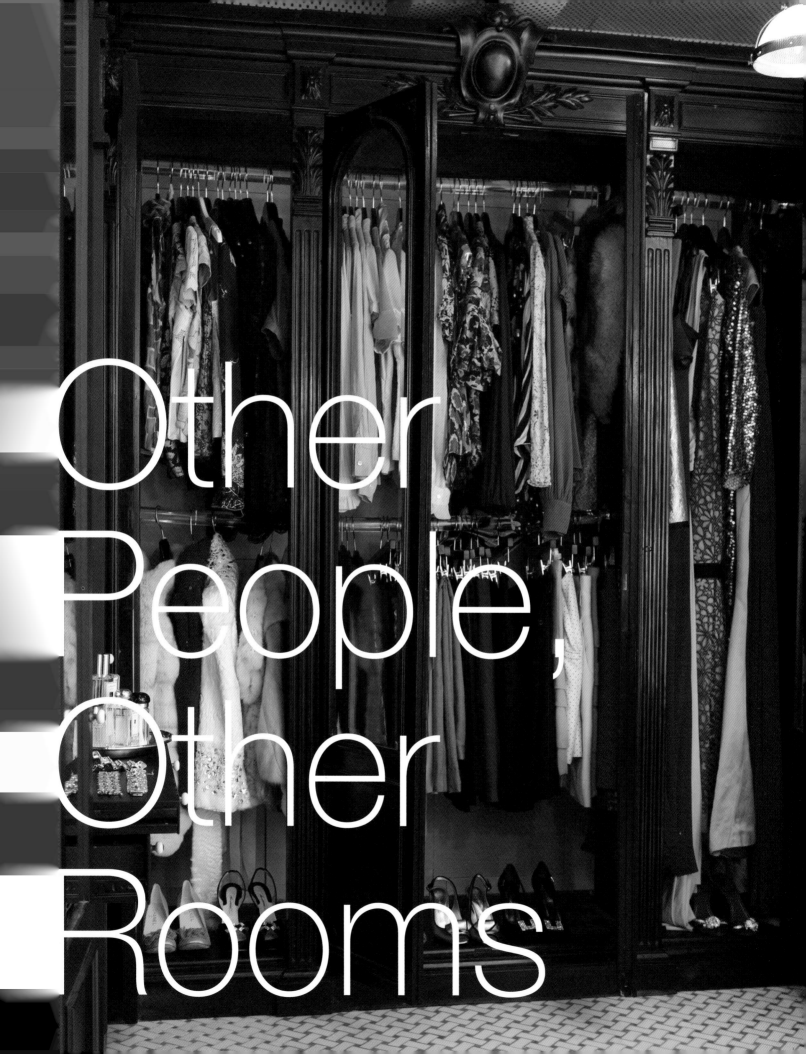

Other People, Other Rooms

Most of us do not live entirely alone in our spaces. Even if we are single, people come in and out of our homes, and if we want to be gracious hosts, good friends, and loving partners, we have to accommodate them. A house should reflect our needs and tastes while feeling inviting to friends and family. But how do we do that without settling for the mediocrity that often results from "design by committee"? How do you preserve coherence, distinctiveness, and self-expression while still allowing for compromise?

Sparks Fly:
BOY MEETS GIRL AND COMPROMISE

OPPOSITE
The application of decadent finishes in a basement turns what seems like the booby prize space into one of the most exciting rooms in the house. As shown on page 199, the media and music room, bar, and wine cellar went below ground, where the lack of windows is an advantage. On page 200, the husband's office/paneled library remained upstairs, where the same attention to detail (warped restoration glass in the door) gives great significance to the smallest room in the house.

Trying to incorporate everyone's fantasy into one room does not work. When couples embark on decorating a new room, the girls usually win. Even couples who have been happy with their rooms for a long time can suddenly find themselves eager for a fresh start—and in my experience it tends to be women who instigate the process. Initially the husband balks, not wanting to sacrifice his favorite chair, but it often turns out that he is hungry for a change, too. (If your experience contradicts my gender generalizations, which practice has proven hold a grain of truth, please forgive me the clichés and adjust the pronouns to suit your situation.)

If your husband insists on a television in the living room or a big leather club chair in the den, there are ways to make the compromise less painful. Disguise the TV (see Chapters 4, 5, and 6) and bring in a new leather chair in a fun color or a beautiful shape instead of the usual brown overscaled marshmallow.

This may put me at risk of sounding stuck in the 1950s, but my observation is that most men have a collection of hobbies that are irreconcilable with the concept of the "pretty room." If you have the space, it may be wise to surrender one room to your partner completely rather than attempt to incorporate his demands or requirements throughout the house in scattered bits and pieces. A basement or an attic can be transformed into a "man room" where he can enjoy the more unattractive tools of his trade that often relate to sports, music, or media. The good news is that most men just want a private room where design is at a minimum and they can pursue their pastimes in privacy and peace. (Women usually want the same but with design at a maximum.) Amazingly, lack of windows and lots of quiet can actually be an asset in the male version of this situation.

On the other hand, some historically "masculine" concerns, like wine or book collections, backgammon or chess tables, and reading chairs are beautiful in their own right and add elegant integrity of purpose when melded into dining rooms, living rooms, and other family areas.

Many men are very happy living in spaces women have designed, maybe because feminine rooms tend to be traditional, and men relate to tradition. However, demands for total capitulation can engender resentment. Often the best resolution is to subtly weave common masculine elements into graceful and glamorous spaces. Masculinity should manifest itself in details of tailoring (nail heads, lack of flounces and skirts), colors, and textures instead of an overarching design theme.

When I was first married, we faced the "his/mine/ours" furniture-integration problem, which was admittedly exacerbated by the controlling-designer problem (mine)—and our joint tendency to hoard and sentimentalize everything. Constant shopping and rethinking on my end, and a heap of semiexpensive, very traditional antiques auction "victories" on his end have taken several years to sort out. Old pieces that could not be incorporated around the house are on indefinite loan to family members or have been put back on the block.

Some of the "before marriage" pieces that stayed with us are terrific (an enormous sofa, a wooden wine shelf, a collection of volcano paintings, and a double-sided metal library bookcase); others represent unresolved issues and call for high tolerance levels from both of us. The baby grand piano in our living room is one such example, and I fear there will be no happy ending to its story in the foreseeable future. My husband bought it in a swell of charming enthusiasm. He thought he would learn to play it, but to my ear as well as his, he confesses, he has yet to attain that goal. So there it looms, in the corner of our not-particularly-large living/dining room semihiding the kitty litter box and children's toys I have stashed under its mass. We've had maybe three or four of those magical nights where friends sat down to play an impromptu song, but I suffer an overpowering, almost daily fantasy of waving it good-bye.

I have dreams about how I would use the space if the piano weren't there. I'd place a canopied daybed in that corner, which would sit in the cross section of two windows with two spectacular views. It could be a place of repose and architectural interest . . . and a place for a guest to crash for the night. Or I would install a banquette there for cocktails or dinner-party overflow. But even designers must compromise on design integrity. And in this instance I think I've just plain lost—the piano remains, parked like a big, black SUV or a lacquered hippopotamus in our living room, awaiting the attention of our infant son.

If someone in your house, including yourself, wants to buy a large instrument (or anything large and expensive, for that matter) because someday it *might* get some use, my advice is don't buy it; rent it. If possible, the instrument and the player should have their own room for practice, especially if the person intends to spend more time practicing than "playing." For those who find themselves living with someone who desperately wants a piano (or a bass or a drum set), find a way to make room for it. I was able to help a client whose husband composes and plays music. With three children in the house, only their bedroom offered the solitude, though not really the ideal space, for his instrument and accoutrements. With careful consideration and the tightest paring down of equipment, his wife, while compromising only a bit on her personal space in the room, built a place for him by one of the two windows, to practice and write his music.

Sentiment or guilt about certain pieces of furniture can be overwhelming, and trying to part with them becomes impossible. Don't despair, though, because you can find a solution for living with these inevitable hangers-on. When a piece looks out of sync with your prevailing furniture style, you can overcome the incongruity by marrying them through the use of fabric,

BELOW
Yes, that is a kitty-litter box hiding below our piano, emblem of a marital/design stalemate (of the past five years) still unresolved as of publication; a window seat is used to house a client's keyboard.

OPPOSITE
Lux details (mosaic, copper, and ornate trim) make this basement media room/wine cellar a jewel box, not a subterranean afterthought.

*The two ameoba-shaped
handmade birch bark
headboards fit against a
small wall and are cut and
shaped to allow the light
switch to work.*

paint, or finish. If your inherited side table isn't ideal, cover it with a cloth. Or put an imperfect table on wheels so it can be moved in and out of a room with ease, or skirt it or lacquer it a fresh color. Different styles of upholstered furniture can be redone in the same fabric for a unified but not matching look—if they are of similar scale. But some discords are impossible to paper (or upholster) over. No matter how you upholster a huge club chair, it will always look out of context next to a dainty vintage settee. In that case, a choice has to be made and one of the pieces has to go.

A common scenario happens with hand-me-downs. People incorporate a relative's "off" piece into a room while continuing to develop a coherent design voice around it. Over time, the more they refine their taste and acquisitions, the quality of the room rises to such a level that the sentimental furnishing is shackling an ever-evolving scheme. Finally, they can let it go.

THIS PAGE AND OPPOSITE
These "rooms" (including a closet-turned-wine-tasting-room) have thought-out design and character but gender-neutral tailoring and color palettes to make both halves of a couple happy.

This is why I tell couples not to keep the train in the design station just because they are fighting about one or two pieces (or ideas). Stops along the way are inevitable, so I advise clients to just get going and not let Granny's sideboard distract from or delay the project. The fact is that while proceeding with a scheme, tastes will likely evolve. Like the body, rooms tend to heal themselves in time if taken care of. The key is not to let the offending element adversely influence the entire room or drive the selection process for the enduring elements. You may be better off simply accepting the piece's existence but designing around it, as if it didn't exist.

A couple's lifestyle differences, like aesthetic ones, can also complicate design decisions. For example, one person's desire to put his feet up on a coffee table may conflict with the other person's taste for soft woods, Lucite, or lacquer. This is a challenge I face at home. We entertain frequently and host fund-raisers and political parties; we have kids and pets; and the two of us occasionally act like messy children ourselves. My husband does not want anything in the house that he has to worry about getting stained or broken or stolen at the expense of being able to use our house freely to celebrate the causes, events, and candidates we care about. I agree with him, but I also work in a business that involves the pursuit of beautiful, occasionally fragile objects, under whose spell I often fall. We looked at our real priorities and chose to create a house in which we hope never to say, "No, don't put a glass there" (we are not coaster people), or "No, don't go in that room," and so on. I have found a coffee table with a glass top, brass sides, and Lucite details. Finally. Even with feet on it, our coffee table looks like jewelry to me.

The key to preventing design disasters and endless arguments over the relative merits of each individual decision is to create overarching rules. Every design choice we now make follows our "coffee table guidelines"—color, pleasing scale, and interesting pattern are essential, and pieces must be made in a material that appeals to me but is rugged enough to handle feet, glasses, kids, dogs, and careless people. Designing with uniformly industrial-strength textiles makes a house look institutional and drab, so for soft furnishings, such as club chairs and pillows, I indulged in the use of more delicate materials. I also contracted with a company called

Fiber-Seal to provide us with a protective coating on our upholstery. I have just crossed my fingers and gone on enjoying my red wine.

Firsthand professional experience has shown me some design marriages made in heaven. A few couples who were not united in their design vision were at least capable of effective discourse. Ideally, a couple should be able to look at everything they have, pinpoint what works, and eliminate the rest. One couple I work with has a particularly sensible communication system worked out. Knowing that at times they will reach impasses, they hired me to act as impartial tiebreaker and facilitator. They wisely realized how hard it is to share decision-making equitably if one person in the partnership is more responsible for the implementation. This role of arbitrator can be outsourced to a trusted and impartial friend, though a nonprofessional may be less likely to offer several equally "correct" solutions.

Children and Their Rooms

The desire to include children in all aspects of family life can mean that every corner of your house looks like a nursery school. Even those lucky few who have the luxury of a separate play area often end up with big blue trucks and brilliantly colored block sets rolling and tumbling through their living rooms. As toys overtake the entire house, hiding and storing the evidence of youth becomes a primary concern.

Boxes and baskets can neatly hold toys on a shelf or under a console table in public areas, such as living and family rooms. Big skirted tables, so long as they are stable in their own right and weighted down with a heavy glass top, are also very kid friendly. Children's paraphernalia can be stashed underneath a skirted table so it's invisible yet available.

Be especially practical in play areas, and think ottomans (with built-in storage). A tray on top provides the hard, flat surface adults need for drinks, books, etc. if the ottoman is replacing a coffee table. Kids also like to lean on things and push them around—and out of their way—as they career about. So, use three or four smaller ottomans that can be easily moved. Low stools work well as extra adult seating and, for kids, as seats and tables.

LEFT
Tried-and-true bunk beds are an exciting, fun, ideal use of space, allowing children more play room.

OPPOSITE
Bright or primary-colored rooms go a long way when housing toys, which tend to be of the same colors. Pastel baby rooms become incongruous with growing children's gear. In my son's room, we upholstered the walls, chair, and crib in bright green faux leather both because I love the color and because of its usefulness in mess prevention. The dark rug shows fuzz balls so it appreciates frequent vacuuming but spills have been of no consequence.

OPPOSITE AND THIS PAGE
Custom details in children's bedrooms, such as faux painting on steps, whimsically painted walls, mismatched lampshades, wallpaper-starred ceilings, a tailored daybed, or carefully matched curtains and bedding make tiny clutter-filled rooms more orderly but still a lot of fun.

Choose upholstery fabric for durability so you won't be gnashing your teeth when your kid spills cranberry juice. I use faux leather, Ultrasuede, and slipcovers liberally in children's areas.

Bedrooms for children should be energetic, exciting, and filled with their personality. When selecting colors, keep in mind what you're up against. Kids need visual stimulation and amusement; adults need coherence and refuge. The primary-colored plastic cars, trucks, dolls, music machines, bouncies, and blocks that inevitably become "accessories" in a child's room are visually loud and demanding. They ultimately overpower or overwhelm a pastel room. Bearing this in mind, we upholstered my son's room in lime green faux leather—and accessorized with similarly bright artwork, lamps, and, of course, those toys.

Parents often ask if they should let children pick their design scheme. I think it is okay as long as the parameters are tight. If you bring a child to a wall of paint chips and say, pick one, he or she will be completely overwhelmed (and more often than not will choose the brightest neon purple on the rack). To make them feel a part of the process, give them a choice of three preapproved colors and two styles of furniture. Or select your materials and technique and ask them if there is an element or theme they have seen in a book or movie that delights them. One client's child answered, *The Little Mermaid* and was thrilled when her bathroom was painted as an underseascape; it wasn't necessary to turn it into a theme park featuring Sebastian, Ariel, Ursula, and Flounder. The daughter felt as if she had made an important

Art Show

Go bold and whimsical with art in children's and baby's rooms. For example, one-color paintings or silhouette drawings are fun to look at: white flowers against brown paper bag material, or yellow animals against blue kraft paper. If you can think ahead, give your child paints in colors you want to use in their room and let them have at it with a blank canvas. The result will be an abstract masterpiece; a slightly parent-engineered colorfield painting. Frame old children's greeting cards or plates from books for instant kid-friendly and inexpensive art. Or custom paint details on unexpected places on the wall (low enough for pint-sized viewing), instead of doing massive murals. Children want and want, but are often just as excited by a little as a lot.

contribution, and her parents had artfully dodged the commercial cliché bullet. In general, I recommend making reference to a "theme" in only the subtlest of ways. Children are hard-wired to exuberantly embrace themes as they do a catchy new tune, but as with the latest song, even your child will tire of it quickly and with a finality that is astounding.

I created a toy soldier–themed room for a pair of boys just out of their cribs, but again it was done in traditional style, and it was not tied to a brand or a cartoon character that the boys would grow bored with. Instead, the inspiration was a classic wooden soldier owned by their grandmother, which we had wired as a lamp that sat on a red wicker table between the boys' twin beds. The palette was patriotic. No baby colors, but bright, cracking blues and reds and a crisp white. The boys' mother liked the graphic idea of that color trio and the result was a very stylish and sophisticated room, but still perfect for boys. We used a lot of white-painted furniture from off-the-rack sources. The only custom touch was a trunk at the end of each bed. They were hand painted with soldiers.

Matchy-matchy works especially well in babies' rooms and nurseries because infants represent (wonderful) exhaustion and bewilderment. A room that is very simple and coordinated, with a limited palette of three colors, acts as a calming influence. In one Manhattan nursery I used the same graphic brown and cream Lela's rose pattern of my own design on the nursing chair, stool, and draperies. The wall was painted in a very neutral pink and the furnishings, including the crib, were done in crisp white. A clear Lucite console became a changing table set against the window with a skyline view high above the city. The overall effect was serene but sophisticated.

Wall-to-wall carpet is the most sensible floor covering for children's and infant's bed- and play-rooms. For softness and durability, wool carpets are best. The newest wool and polypropylene blends are almost impermeable to stains and look like sisal and feel good underfoot. They aren't quite as soft as wool, but they are more tolerant of accidents—bring out the crayons and the ink gun. If you are going to upholster a chair, Ultrasuede or faux leather is best. Chalkboard paint is great—cover a wall with it, so everyone has a permissible place to draw. Or use large-scale decorative stickers for temporary pizzazz.

Consider using daybeds that allow you to employ the nursery as a place for a catnap during night feedings, a place where toddlers and children can sleep.

Children's rooms require the same variety of lighting as any room, but standing and table lamps must be secured so they do not topple over. I cut out huge pieces of extrastrength Velcro, adhere them under the lamp bases, and stick them to the floor or side tables. Of course, when you tear off the industrial-strength adhesive when your son or daughter is old enough, it may remove much of the paint from the table. Standing lamps can sit in a corner with a reading chair backed into them so they are secure and their wires are out of reach. Recessed lights, wall sconces, and picture lights affixed to bookshelves are the safest course of action.

Children are hard-wired to exuberantly embrace themes as they do a catchy new tune, but as with the latest song, even your child will tire of it quickly and with a finality that is astounding.

Overnight Guests

OPPOSITE AND BELOW
Whether your guest room provides an excuse to indulge whimsical design fantasy or hotel-like efficiency, these spaces speak volumes about your eagerness to provide guests with a comfortable experience.

Single-function guest rooms are wonderful oases and fantasy spaces clean from the clutter of necessity and daily life—stock them with a few recent best sellers, a water glass and carafe, soft sheets on a comfortable bed, cozy blankets, and soft down pillows, and most visitors will be very happy. However, if you are one of the many who lack the space for such a luxury and must have convertibility, I am a big believer in the small-space living philosophy of investing in the best pullout couch you can find for your den or family room. Even if you have loads of spare bedrooms, there's always a need for a dual-purpose room, especially if you have college-aged children who are apt to bring home extra friends for weekend visits.

American Leather makes an excellent version that sleeps like a real bed. Its patented mechanism does not create that awkward gap between the mattress and the back of the sofa and it projects about 10 to 12 inches *less* than most sofa beds into the room, making it extremely space efficient. I have one in my den and my guests say it is like sleeping on a conventional mattress. Because I wanted a different style than the company offered, I splurged and remade the frame around the mechanism. Daybeds are also terrific solutions for guest quarters because, when pushed lengthwise against a wall or under a window and filled with pillows, they can be used as a sofa.

BELOW
In this Adirondack great room, furniture of varying scales and styles, and castoff pieces assembled from multiple other houses, coexist comfortably because they are unified in the eclectic setting and red and brown color story.

LEFT
We matched the majority of the upholstery to the fur color of the owner's Chihuahua, a tiny but prolific shedder.

Pets

Pets aren't exactly "people too" but they are part of many lives and families, including my own. Assuming your dog or cat is fully potty trained, you can educate your pet to live within the confines of your life. The biggest problems tend to involve scratching, fur, and the general digestive and scatological messes of puppydom and old age. One client of mine put tin foil on the sofa (lending a Warhol's-factory look) where her kitties liked to claw. They hated the feel of it and the memory has not faded, so now, even though the foil has long since been removed, they won't go anywhere near it. She also cut a panel out of her utility closet and placed the kitty litter inside as a clever way to disguise the inevitable. Dog and cat doors are brilliant for letting creatures come and go at will.

To solve the hair issue, buy at least two inexpensive throws in a color you like, and place them on sofas and chairs where pets like to perch. Remove them when you are in presentation mode, and swap them once a week to wash. The Gonzo Sponge is a fantastic product for removing pet hair and lint. Just rub it over the offending patch of upholstery, and it draws the fur into one giant easily removable "pill." In terms of fabrics, if you are totally devoted to your white dog, don't get a dark velvet sofa and vice versa. Very few materials are completely fur resistant, but faux leather has proven an all-around animal pleaser. After countless years trying to clear pet hair–clogged vacuum cleaner bags, I was thrilled when Dyson invented the solution. In my opinion, it's the best vacuum cleaner there is for eliminating pet hair.

Is Everyone Having Fun?

We do a lot of entertaining—but very rarely in a formal way. In an effort to adhere to formality or convention, most people hold events that are labor intensive, time-consuming, and expensive, but ordinary. I prefer to make 99 percent of my party as simple and easy as possible, reserving my free time and budget to make the last 1 percent wonderful and unique, because people always remember the figurative "candy." For instance, I'd rather serve dinner on paper plates but follow it with a bottle of spectacular Sauternes. Or I'd forget the expensive flower budget and wow them with an abundance of firelight—a gratuitous number of votive candles (which store easily). Skip the napkin rings and the elaborate or exotic food and blow your budget on Mount Vesuvius as the birthday cake. The party will be more spirited and the photos more fantastic sans formality and formula.

I find big buffets, hors d'oeuvres, or picnic parties to be more fun and easier than formal sit-down dinners, even though many more guests participate. That's because of the way we do it: self-serve and no bartender (people get trapped in the drink throng in front of a service bar). We fill big buckets with ice and bottles (beer, wine, water, soda) and have a table full of stemware and glasses. We serve one special mixed drink to people as they come in—after that they fend for themselves. Everyone seems to like it that way—no waiting is necessary and people feel less passive about their role at the party. If you have a good friend who drinks only Scotch, have a bottle for him in the kitchen and let him know it's there. People love to have special privileges in your house—they sometimes feel most welcome when exercising this familiarity.

If you enjoy entertaining on a large scale frequently, have your own inexpensive supplies at the ready if you have room to store them. Renting glassware gets expensive, the coordination is tedious, and lugging rental house crates in and out is more work and wear and tear on your house than you realize. Crate & Barrel stacking glasses—thin, big, versatile, beautiful and, at a few dollars each, affordable—are the workhorses of our parties. We bought more than two hundred of them for less than the price of a few rental charges. Stemless wineglasses are an underrated boon to the hostess—less breakage results because they are so stable, and people are happy to have something in their hands that houses wine as well as Diet Coke. They require less storage space, and most important, they fit en masse in the dishwasher. Champagne can be served in stemless glasses, too. Small, colorful Moroccan tea glasses also work beautifully for champagne; they're irreverently festive, bright, and memorable.

Consider selecting furniture that accommodates expanding crowds or accessories that cater to the party and add utility or beauty to daily life. A modular coffee table can be used in one piece for entertaining a group seated on the sofa, or it can be broken down into smaller tables and placed around the room for a stand-up event. Collect folding chairs and tables and a mix of optional tablecloths over time to allow for impromptu expansion. Pull-up chairs and ottomans help turn an intimate party for two into a shindig for family and friends.

Scent and Sensibility

Don't forget about fragrance—aside from scented candles, boiling orange peels or ginger on the stovetop creates a welcome aroma. As for floral arrangements, I like giant clusters of one kind of bloom and am just as happy with arrangements of branches as I am with delicate flowers.

OPPOSITE

At most parties in our house, everyone but the wily Anchovie (photographed on countertop exile to prevent her from eating low-lying canapés) is allowed to serve him- or herself, so we make frequent use of scattered wine and champagne buckets. Our extra wine is stored in vintage champagne turners mounted on our bar wall—perfect for easy grabbing.

Leave No Surface Untouched

When it's not dressed for a meal, a dining table needs something beautiful on top so it doesn't look like an operating table awaiting a patient. Large lanterns, a huge bowl or tureen, or even a sculptural vase filled with flowers liven up the landscape. I keep a bouquet of preserved flowers on my tabletop. Many designers, weary of dried roses and lavender, put this in their Top 10 Don't lists, but unconventional arrangements of preserved artichokes, poppies, curly willow, and other odd but natural elements give your table low-maintenance charm, not bed-and-breakfast pallor. Don't be insecure—if you like eucalyptus or ceramics, find a way to make them work for you. Another way to exploit an underused dining or occasional table is to place a puzzle in the works on top of a board so it can be pulled, in progress but intact, from the table.

Gifts That Keep Giving

Beautiful old ice buckets or trays are great to collect and give as gifts. You can use the ice buckets for flower arrangements—and of course to hold ice or wine when you entertain. Pretty serving platters or trays are especially useful because you can press them into service elsewhere around the house when not in party mode. After passing the chicken and asparagus on one, you can use it as an after-dinner cheese plate or as a surface for a clock, water carafe, and eyeglasses in the bedroom.

Food service itself need not be difficult, either. There is no reason to have an omelet station or a pasta bar where people end up waiting around, getting taken out of circulation. Have a barbecue instead, with lots of hearty sandwiches, or a big sliced roast and bowls full of tossed salad—all laid out on folding tables adorned with inexpensive lengths of pretty fabric straight from the bolt.

For those who don't love to cook, order out something cheap and simple. Better that than slaving away all day on an exotic menu only to reach a point of resentment by the time your guests arrive. If cooking is part of the fun, choose dishes that can be served in quantity at room temperature so there's no time pressure. Sit back and relax! Make it easy enough so *you* can enjoy the party. Few people want to be around the hostess who has reached her limit when the punch bowl sloshes into the potted palm, no matter how great the room looks.

When I do invite friends for a sit-down meal, I keep it small—six or eight is perfect; more creates fragmented conversations and challenging logistics. Wine and water glasses; a charger; and dinner, salad, and dessert plates complete each setting.

Your home is not a museum or a store. For those who love great design, turning your place into an exhibition space can be tempting. Make every inch of your house hospitable before you concern yourself with formality. Your home should invite everyone who experiences it to feel happy, wanted, *and* aesthetically nourished. Welcoming others into your home, accommodating family members, and entertaining is not about perfection; nor is it a competition. The best novels are about good characters, not just beautiful words. Likewise, the power of good design is shown in how it makes people feel and behave, not how well great objects are assembled. The key is love, friendship, and sharing what you have with others.

Evolving Lives, Changing Tastes

Chapter Eight

1980s

2008

Creating a room is like building a wardrobe—you put on the basics first (in a room, it's the paint, rugs, and big pieces of furniture), then add the accessories (occasional seating, pillows, objects, artwork, and ornament). The accessories steer the look in one direction or another. Yet in other ways, home design is different from dress style.

Fashion in clothing changes from season to season, and the most stylish indulge in a regularly changing wardrobe. The shift may be dramatic—one year the grace of classic Parisian black and white may feel entirely you, then the next a bohemian-gypsy-jewelry-belted-blousy jewel-toned tunic and peg-legged pants may brazen their way into your closet and your self-definition. Even those of us who resist chasing every runway trend participate in the evolution of self that fashion allows. This is not just aesthetic but psychological. There is a natural tension between the desire to affiliate with others and the desire to strike out as individuals. Like clothing styles, home accessories and fabrics evolve inside a cycle where a new "look" moves gradually from innovative and ultramodern, to wildly accepted, to overplayed, dull, or cliché.

Yet even the most avant-garde fashion innovators offer simultaneous common threads of design ideas. On the runway or in the workroom, competitive and autonomous designers often present similar silhouettes or color palettes. A collective unconscious affects the look and themes that cast our lives. That's why artists and architects go in and out of vogue, the vernacular of design changes, new materials develop, and old ones are revived.

Room design trends, fortunately, do not change so frequently and so completely. Instead, we may change the room's "shoes" or "earrings" or "overcoat" often but keep the same "basic black dress" and "suit" for years. A strong basic room design offers not only continuity, but also economy due to its longevity. Due to both physical decay and expected obsolescence of style, the life of a fabric and color scheme is about fifteen years—even if you move more often than that (the best rooms can be transported or repurposed). Without a wholesale change in lifestyle, you can expect a majority of furniture pieces and even well-made (with a 9-inch double hem, which allows 18 inches of additional height for alterations later and extends the usefulness of your curtains), curtains to weather these changes for the long haul.

In the meantime, children are born, jobs change, marriages evolve (or dissolve), new friends are made, experience makes us wiser—and all of it shifts our perspective and alters our taste. Or we just get bored with our environment and want a new outlook. Life happens. We buy a new sofa, update a coffee table, upgrade a rug, or repaint the walls in a more up-to-the-minute color. And who can resist moving around tables and lamps, rearranging sofas and chairs, and editing accessories?

My family home in Palm Beach is the perfect example of this. For more than thirty years, many of its defining design elements (color and light) and stylistic bones, or essence, have remained the same. Pale pink paint still covers the walls and the Portuguese tiles still grace the porch floor. My parents may have considered the pink-and-green pattern a fashionable indulgence in 1974, but that combination has become one of the core defining details of the Old Church. Couches, chairs, fabrics, and accessories have come and gone, of course, but there is tremendous continuity in the house—it has never really changed its fundamental feeling or style. It remains eclectic, humorous, and in many ways traditional, mostly due to the furnishings and

OPPOSITE
From storage facility, to roller-skating rink (the skates in the foreground of the top picture date back to my days of worshipping Tootie from The Facts of Life*), to living room, the nave of the Bethesda-by-the-Sea Church has gone through many transformations, though it still remains a casual, flexible space and repository of family collections, furniture, and memories. The top image shows the space in the 1980s and the bottom in the current decade; see pages 22–23 for its '90s incarnation.*

1980s

1970s

2008

*A collective uncon-
scious affects the
look and themes that
cast our lives.*

OPPOSITE
*The same pink porch, circa
1970s, 1980s, and 2008.*

THIS PAGE
*My great-grandmother
Lucile Lacoste still watches
over the house.*

color scheme. If anything, it has only developed, but its personality is unchanged, as life in the house has progressed.

I have worked on and off with a certain couple over the last seven years whose residence typifies the evolving home. I met them right after she had their first baby and they were moving from a tiny apartment on the Upper West Side of Manhattan to a larger loft in Tribeca. Initially, I helped them evaluate the furniture they owned to figure out what could stay and what should go, and advised them on new pieces to replace those that were not making the move. That was phase one.

When they moved into the then newly built apartment building, we tailored the closet space to create an office that afforded a workroom retreat from the communal living room and dining room. Years after the financial stretch of their initial purchases (almost a full apartment's worth of furniture, wallpaper, and painting at once, then later cabinetry and storage), their budget allowed for the renovation of the standard-issue bathrooms and kitchen. The birth of their third child required converting the office to a nursery and further modification of the shrinking living room to accommodate a new office space. Nothing drastic has happened to the couple's original aesthetic point of view, which is transitional/modern, but their needs changed, and their means and family have expanded. Their house does not look completely different; it just keeps getting better and more defined. My responsibility as a designer was to help them identify what in each phase of their home was merely cool and current (quirky upholstery fabric, trendy accessories) and what would hold true to their household, family, and personal-style ethics over time (large furniture pieces, rugs).

RIGHT

This photo is starting to look very chic to me, but it's a 1970s rendition of a room that has since been entirely transformed. Almost every piece of furniture has been reused someplace in the house; for example, the white chest in this photograph can now be seen in the photograph on page 227, where today it sits under my great-grandmother's portrait. And the red upholstered chair is now floral. The sofa lives on in my New York apartment.

1970s

THIS PAGE AND OPPOSITE
This bedroom has transformed through the years. The painting on the walls and floors has changed, as has the orientation of the bed. But vestiges of earlier years remain: The chair in the opposite photograph came from the pink porch shown in the 1970 setting on page 226.

Designing into the Future

In my own home and in my clients', I reuse and transform certain objects and furnishings on a regular basis. They are my "go to" pieces such as the staple English arm sofa that was floral in a single lady's living room, then recovered in leather for her den after she and her husband were married. When you find and fall in love with any of the items described below, *buy them* because you will keep them around your house forever, transforming them when appropriate and finding different uses for them. That's especially valuable for the home that is designed over time. Here's my list of twelve "can't-go-wrong, must-haves" that you will find easy to own and adapt over time.

Coffee Tables

Parsons, lacquered Asian-legged, and glass-topped varieties are my favorites—they can be left as is forever or repainted or refinished to suit a changing palette or décor. Their tops can be either replaced or covered. For instance, switch clear glass with mirrored glass to enhance a casual coffee table's sophistication. Or lay marble or another stone in the glass inset area, or on top of any of these tables to change its look.

Console Tables

Consoles are long, narrow tables designed to be placed against a wall or behind a sofa—the perfect examples of flexibility and utility combined. They have numerous practical uses, from holding decorative items (sculpture, flowers, clocks, books) or lamps to holding writing implements and keys as the perfect entry or hall table or even to serving as a desk (most are wide enough to accommodate a laptop). Those without lower shelves provide a place to tuck ottomans under when not in use. Consoles can double as a room divider as well—visually separating dining and living areas in great rooms, or living and sleeping areas in studio apartments.

Hold Those Thoughts

Keep good records and material samples. Receipts that contain important product information may otherwise get tossed in a desk drawer purge. An overzealous Sunday-afternoon garage-cleaning binge results in paint cans being pitched. An enthusiastic closet reorganization may resign upholstery fabric remnants to the dustbin—months before a leak leaves a sofa cushion irreversibly stained. The solution does not require a complex series of files or scrapbooks. Keep in an envelope or notebook even postage-stamp–size samples of all elements you use in every room—the paint brushed on a card with the name of the color, number of coats, and the manufacturer's ID number; fabric and trim stapled to its vendor's business card. Then, if you plan to continue shopping over the years, you can use these elements to make a separate cheat sheet with the colors of each room stapled to or painted on a smaller piece of card stock so that you have a travel-sized palette to refer to. This will also prevent you from raiding and dismantling your master file.

While you're at it, stuff receipts and cards from shops, manufacturers, craftsmen, and contractors into a manila folder. Receipts often have measurements noted on them. If you want to make a matching twin slipcover for your sofa a couple of years down the road, it helps. Even if you are returning to the same manufacturer, they may have gotten rid of your records. Knowing exact date of manufacture and dimensions can help them resurrect original templates. And, when the time comes to list your items on eBay, you will have all relevant information at your fingertips.

Go Versatile

I love pieces that have modular qualities and multiple functions so much that I have produced the following in my line of furniture with Laneventure. The concept, not the brand, is important:

• Two or more serpentine chests of drawers that make a huge buffet when pushed together.

• Twenty-four-inch–wide armless dining chairs with a matching corner piece. They can be lined up along a wall to make a banquette, or broken up to be used as chairs for a dinner party, or you can face two of the corner pieces away from each other to make a tête-a-tête.

• Wooden cubes, garden seats, or small and sturdy 18-inch high side tables in multiples (two, four, or six) can be configured into a coffee table. They can also work as a whimsical bench at the foot of a bed, as low bedside tables, as a convenient surface between two chairs, or as seats and storage for children's rooms.

• Any piece of furniture that converts from one purpose to another, such as a desk that transforms into a coffee table (like my campaign table/file cabinet), lamp tables or coffee tables that turn into dining tables, or dining tables that second as desks or sofa tables.

• Slipper chairs—small-scale chairs without arms—take up less space, but they are tailored and pretty.

• Swivel chairs are fun, sexy, and useful.

RIGHT
A campaign-style filing cabinet flips open to become a desk—perfect for many uses and for spaces that evolve over time.

A Pair of Club Chairs

Club chairs offer comfort, mobility, and a beautiful smaller-size body for your favorite upholstery fabric, have a strong silhouette, and can define a room even in the early stages of decorating. They also happen to be the most comfortable secondary seating in any room. If you don't have space for a couch, find two small club chairs instead. In larger spaces, a grouping of four around a coffee table makes for a conversation area with a library feel. Flanking a fireplace, a matched pair creates intimate seating or reading areas.

Nesting Tables

These sets are very practical for spaces large and small. Tucked together, or pulled slightly out so the two lower-height levels protrude from under the main table, nesting tables tuck nicely next to a sofa or chair and provide variable heights and just enough surface for a lamp, a book, and a cup of tea. Placed against a wall, they can act as a small console and then be pressed into service for impromptu dinners in front of the fire (or TV); they are perfect for small apartments with no room for traditional dining facilities.

Trunks

Easy to find at vintage stores, garage sales, and flea markets, trunks and chests beautifully serve their original purpose—storage—at the foot of a bed or under a window. They can also work double duty as a seat or bench. When using one as a coffee table, keep it shallow so that it can be raised off the floor to allow for feet to slide comfortably beneath.

Large Table Lamp

You can employ a bold and unusual table lamp as the "statement" piece in an otherwise simple space, and can introduce an interesting material—Murano glass, metal design, ceramic, stone, wood—where you need it. Configure an odd lamp from found objects—children's toys, antique canisters, baskets, sculpture (that is not valuable), or vases. Pairs of lamps behind a sofa lend near-instant symmetry to a room.

Bookcases

Whether the least expensive IKEA shelving unit brimming with paperbacks or an architectural masterpiece carefully filled with leather-bound volumes, bookcases always add life, height, and character to a room. A well-used bookcase offers heft, stability, backbone, character, and a sense of life lived. Not only do the cases hold books, but they also offer hideaways for sentimental but clutter-y items in boxes or baskets or closed shelves; and pretty places to casually display family photos, art, and favorite objects. Backless bookcases make great room dividers because they do not totally block light or views; they just obscure them. Bookcases add instant architecture where none exists, a multiplicity of color through all the book spines, and, if they are lit, a wonderful source of indirect illumination in a room. I consider them fully outfitted when dressed not only with books and art, but when the interior backing has a special treatment such as cockerel or a small-patterned paper, a mirror, or a leather lining.

OPPOSITE ABOVE RIGHT
AND LEFT AND THIS PAGE
*Grass-cloth walls and
painted floors always make
me happy! They add texture,
charm and color.*

OPPOSITE BELOW
*A mirrored screen hides air
conditioning/heating vents
and reflects light and view
from opposing windows.*

Screens

The perfect meeting of art and functionality, screens are both beautiful to look at and highly efficient. Because they are so mobile, you can move them wherever they need to be whenever they need to be there. They act as room dividers as well as add height to a space. Hand-painted, rare, or otherwise exceptional examples can be hung on a wall as art, making a grand statement behind a couch or on a large expanse of wall. Other, less valuable examples make for corner softeners and allow boxy rooms to feel less cubic. Employ them to hide all your "scaries and uglies," like stacking chairs, the kitty litter box, hideous plastic playthings, or pedestrian radiators and air-conditioning intake grates—even unattractive galley kitchens in small apartments. (For examples, see pages 161, 188, 198, and 238.) Best of all, simple trifold screens are easy to customize—they can be upholstered, wallpapered, mirrored, or painted.

Trays and Baskets

Instead of a home office, create a home office basket or tray and take your berries, pods, and laptops into the quietest room in the house to work or listen or play. Keeping a tray next to the bed means you can bus your midnight musings, water glass, and books from room to room the next day. A basket in the front hall acts as a shopping cart and mail or key ring and clutter holder. On side tables and coffee tables, a tray corrals disparate objects and unifies them. Many trays and baskets are so beautiful and decorative they can stand alone as three-dimensional wall or table art. Look for antique or vintage ones in a variety of materials (shagreen, parchment, silver, enamel) or spray paint dull trays and baskets with a popping color or line them with fabric. Personalize baskets by stenciling names or purposes on their sides.

Secretary or Tall Étagère

Nothing adds stature to a space like an elegant secretary or étagère. True servants of a room, they hold precious objects and keepsakes, offer surfaces for a bar or food, and stand in as a place to write and work. They also count as modular because they close up the clutter, so they get three stars, for flexibility, function, and beauty. (See page 205 for an example.)

Wall Upholstery or Wallpaper

Comforting and cozy, wallpaper or battened fabric gives a room a kind of quiet and coherence that no other wall treatment offers. You are truly enveloped in texture, color, and pattern. If covering a large space seems daunting, consider upholstering a niche for a reading alcove.

Bench, Ottoman, or Hassock

Because it's a matter of manners to have another place to sit in the bedroom besides your bed, some sort of seating surface is essential. (Even if your sleeping quarters are minimal, you can probably squeeze in a hassock or a tuft at the foot of the bed or in a corner near a window.) Portable and easy to hide, small seating surfaces cheerfully fit into small bath—and bedrooms. An extra seat in the bathroom can act as a step stool to reach up into the linen closet or a place to sit while bathing or drying off a child. If space allows, team a single matching ottoman with a pair of club chairs in the bedroom to keep the energy in the marriage. This small unifier of a shared ottoman brings two furniture pieces together in a way that signifies enormous comfort.

More Favorite Things . . .

An English-armed sofa

A little bit of animal print in every room

Bamboo or other materials painted, carved, or molded
to look like bamboo

Canopy beds

Lava stone for tabletops

Ikat fabrics

Grass-cloth wall coverings

Portuguese rugs and embroidered bed linens

Natural-fiber rugs—sisal, sea grass, abaca, jute, hemp, wool

Plain sisal rug faux painted in Aubusson style—so chic, it turns
formality on its head by playfully mixing casual material with
traditional pattern and form

Lattice-covered walls, à la Dorothy Draper

The gams on Asian tables—pretty, flirty, feminine, and classic
enough to fit any décor

Clean, uncluttered surfaces—tables not suppressed by piles of paper,
books, magazines, and junk

Extraordinary ceilings—faux painted or wallpapered

Dramatic floors with inlay stone, or faux-painted graphic patterns

Every Designer Has Her Imperious Idiosyncrasies . . .

There are exceptions to every rule, opposition to every opinion. Yet I cannot keep myself from divulging some of my personal design don'ts—which you have permission to laugh off. All designers have them, and mine are no more shocking (yet no less emphatic) than anyone else's. Here are the items, objects, and ideas that I do not think make a positive contribution to a home.

- The ubiquitous dark or jewel-toned reproduction Persian carpet. They appear to me as unsuccessful stabs at formality and opulence. Unless you are in love with your ruby red, gold, and royal blue rug, get rid of it and find one with a softer or less predictable palette. Allow your pillows and walls and fun knickknacks to spread color around a room.

- Too much wall-to-wall carpeting. It's fine in a bedroom or a playroom, but in a living room it feels too casual, dingy, and officelike.

- Mirrors hung horizontally, which foreshorten ceiling height.

- Lacquered brass—it lacks warmth at its most harmless and at its worst, is garish. Like too much plastic surgery, the artifice is more glaring than the perfection achieved.

- Anything that is billed as a "collectible." If the vendor has to suggest the possibility to you, it's probably not worth collecting.

- The word and any object that can be considered a "figurine."

- Overuse of burled wood. Unless it is on an antique, and has earned a soft patina, burled wood looks too much like dictator chic . . . it might work in Dubai or on your private 737, but most likely not in your living room.

- Crystal-encrusted anything.

- Over-the-top grandeur and opulence or attempts at it . . . may be perfect in the château, or an old hotel, or a casino, and even in Trump's lobby, but not at your house.

- The genre of kitsch. Camp does not work for me in any design element. Irony (as in Jonathan Adler) has a lot going for it but kitsch doesn't . . . the idea that there is still humor in a cliché is over (I mean, would you really wear an I'M WITH STUPID T-shirt?). I once dated a guy who had a life-size Yoda in the middle of his apartment, and there was nothing charming about it after the first "You must be kidding."

- Air fresheners—I am almost phobic about plugs-ins and sprays, both of which always have a distinct mix of vanilla and plasticity to their scent. There are plenty of other delicious-smelling alternatives out there.

- Skirted tables of any diameter less than 30 inches look very Little Miss Muffett.

- Beveled mirrors.

- Matching bedroom "suites"—bed, night tables, bureau, and dresser.

- Feather beds that aren't 100 percent down or entirely synthetic. The quills in most feathers are prickly.

Imperfection You Can Live With

A missing knob, a ding or scratch on an antique, chipped glasses, cracks in an old mirror, a bit of peeling paint, a few scuffs or dents on the floor.

Imperfection You Can't Live With

Dirt, grime, fingerprints, grease stains, torn upholstery, dust.

Organization Obsession

I can't live without my P-touch labeler. From putting the color and styles of shoes on foggy plastic shoe boxes to identifying what photos or bills are in which storage box, this little gadget lets me indulge in both procrastination—" I can't go to the gym, I'm labeling!"—and the micromanagement of the inane, as in creating identifying stickers for individual pieces of costume jewelry, vintage tablecloths, or fabric swatches. Well, at least my things are well kept!

Living Luxury

Luxurious living is not about having the most expensive furniture and a fancy address. It's about comfort and happiness. Here, my top personal luxuries (they *never* go out of style):

A bed to dream about. Material, not thread count, creates soft bed linens. Shop by touch more than by thread count because a 600-thread count sheet made from short-fiber cotton is just a lot of mediocre cotton. Soft sheets are made from long fibers, and Egyptian and Pima cotton (also known as Extra Long Staple cotton) has the longest, which soften with every washing. You can also find vintage Egyptian cotton sheets and old linen sheets online, in vintage shops, or at garage sales. If you can sleep in a hotel without fear, you should be able to launder vintage linens and not fret about their previous lives. Embroidery is a whole other load of luxury. Hand-stitched details on dreamy soft sheets and pillows and comforters made of 100 percent down are my most indulgent and intimate luxuries.

Sparkling-clean windows. The view improves considerably when soot and dust are removed. More light filters into rooms, too.

Great-smelling, long-burning candles. Slatkin, Jo Malone, Diptyque, and Manuel Canovas make especially good ones.

Picture frames fitted with antique glass. The way the bubbles and ripples catch the light is unmatched by new glass. And the artwork underneath gets an added old-world glow, too.

A few tiny paintings. Set on easels or placed on small tables, these mini masterpieces are charming. Amateur oils appear regularly on eBay and other online auctions, and at antiques stores and consignment and charity shops.

Antique mirrors. Perhaps not the best for checking yourself out in, but the foggier and more mottled the glass, the more mystery and history they add to a room. Antique mirrors glow more enchantingly in candlelight than brand-new versions.

ABOVE

Long-fiber hand-embroidered bed linens are the ultimate treat. My preference is for white bed linens, but whenever I can, I embellish with hand embroidery or appliqué as shown in these impeccable and luxurious bed linens by Leron.

Last But Not Least

Designing a home is both a form of aesthetic self-expression and an exciting adventure. Many of us travel abroad from time to time to replenish our sense of excitement in the outside world. We devote days, even weeks, to planning a two-week vacation. Why not bring the same energy and sense of possibility to your inside world—to the walls within which you spend most of your time? Your house is your second skin, and the environment you create is an extension of yourself—your ultimate self-portrait. Where we live is who we are.

Coming up with rooms you love isn't easy, but it can be both exhilarating and affirming. The novelist and essayist Alain de Botton, author of *The Architecture of Happiness,* movingly describes the intrinsic joys of beautiful surroundings. A thoughtfully assembled library or light-reflecting material, he writes, can suggest to us "something about patience and stability, tenderness and sweetness, intelligence and worldliness, skepticism and trust."

Your home is one of the few places where you can exercise complete control over your surroundings. Explore your tastes, indulge and comfort yourself, make your home a place where you can replenish your energies time and time again, so you can enjoy the leisure, and even the work, of your daily life. It takes time, care, and thought, but the value of building this second self is lasting.

Think of decorating your house as you might approach assembling a personal art gallery that showcases what matters to you most. Let the walls and furnishings evoke memories of travels, friends, family, and celebrations. I hope this book becomes an atlas of new directions, coaxing you to begin the journey of home design with greater confidence about the terrain, with style and practicality as your compass. Each of you carries within knowledge of the highly individual combination of shapes, colors, textures, and objects that can be used to make your house feel like home. As a designer, my greatest wish is to act as guide . . . to your taste.

Your house is your second skin, and the environment you create is an extension of yourself—your ultimate self-portrait.

OPPOSITE
A bold pattern of limestone inlaid with wood creates a welcoming and dramatic floor in a Palm Beach entryway.

RESOURCES

Building, renovating, refurbishing, design, and decorating are all really just a few clicks away—here is a list of just some of my favorite haunts (I'd need a whole other book to list all of them). Fortunately, the Internet makes it possible for you to access their resources and products no matter where you live. Those with storefronts are worth in-person visits if you happen to be in the neighborhood!

Building and Renovating

Clos-ette
31 Union Square West, 12D
New York, NY 10003
877.803.9797
www.clos-ette.com
Custom closets.

FiberSeal
214.333.9400
www.fiberseal.com
Fabric-care systems available from dealers nationwide.

P.E. Guerin, Inc.
23 Jane Street
New York, NY 10014
212.243.5270
www.peguerin.com
Handmade decorative and architectural hardware.

Red Star Painting
7249 Loubet Street
Flushing, NY 11375
917.226.2961
Professional painting services.

Archie McAlister
Dog Productions Inc.
238 North 9th Street
Brooklyn, NY 11211
718.782.7080
Carpentry.

Ilan Telmont
306 East 11th Street, #4A
New York, NY 10003
917.459.7676
General contractor.

Design and Decorating

ACCESSORIES AND HOME FURNISHINGS

Blackman Cruz
310.657.9228
www.blackmancruz.com
Modern 19th- and 20th-century furnishings.

Cooper-Hewitt Design Museum Shop
2 East 91st Street
New York, NY 10128
212.849.8400
www.cooperhewitt.org

Hunter Douglas
1.800.789.0331
www.hunterdóuglas.com
Window treatments, blinds, and shades at authorized dealers nationwide.

Jarlathdan
303 Main Street
Amagansett, NY 11930
631.267.6455
www.jarlathdan.com
Contemporary furnishings and accessories

Jonathan Adler
8125 Melrose Avenue
Los Angeles, CA 90046
323.658.8390
www.jonathanadler.com
Modern furnishings, accessories, and textiles.

Mary Mahoney
351 Worth Avenue
Palm Beach, FL 33480
561.655.5751
Modern tabletop accessories.

Niermann Weeks
The Fine Arts Building
232 East 59th Street, ground floor
New York, NY 10022
212.319.7979
www.niermannweeks.com
Fine art, lighting, and accessories.

Objects of Design
01.488.71236
www.objects-of-design.com
English retailers of handmade home accessories.

Odegard
212.545.0069
www.odegardinc.com
Stephanie Odegard–designed lighting, textiles, and accessories.

Steven Amadee
41 North Moore Street
New York, NY 10013
212.343.1696
Fine custom framing.

Vivre
800.411.6515
www.vivre.com
Online source for funky, fashionable contemporary home furnishings.

Voltz Clarke Gallery
www.voltzclarke.com
A variety of work by a range of contemporary artists.

ANTIQUE AND VINTAGE

145 Antiques
27 West 20 Street
New York, New York 10011
212.807.1149
www.145antiques.com
Assorted vintage and modern.

Balasses House
208 Main Street
Amagansett, NY 11930
631.267.3032
Antiques and vintage accessories.

CBell Furnishing Life
4906 South Dixie Highway
West Palm Beach, FL 33405
561.533.6505
www.cbellfurnishing.com

Chapman Radcliff
517 North La Cienega Blvd.
West Hollywood, CA 90048
310.659.8062
www.chapmanradcliff.com
Modern furniture and accessories.

Denton and Gardner Ltd.
2491 Main Street
Bridgehampton, NY 11932
631.537.4796
www.dentongardner.com
19th- and 20th-century European and American furniture, paintings, and lighting.

Dolce
3700 S. Dixie Highway, #8
West Palm Beach, FL 33405
561.832.4550

Downtown
719 N. La Cienega Blvd.
Los Angeles, CA 90069
310.652.7461
http://downtown.1stdibs.com/search.php
Modern vintage furniture and accessories

Dragonette Ltd.
711 North La Cienega Blvd.
Los Angeles, CA 90069
310.855.9091
www.dragonetteltd.com
Vintage modern furniture and accessories.

Duane Antiques
176 Duane Street
New York, NY 10013
212.625.8066
www.duaneantiques.com
Vintage modern furniture and accessories.

Fat Chance
162 North La Brea Avenue
Los Angeles, CA 90036
323.930.1960
www.fatchancemodern.com
Modern vintage furniture and accessories.

1stdibs.com
www.1stdibs.com
Internet clearinghouse for mid-century modern furniture from a variety of dealers.

GoAntiques.com
www.goantiques.com
Online source for vintage art, accessories, and antiques.

Home Anthology
www.homeanthology.com
Deco, mid-century, and vintage furniture, lighting, and accessories.

Harris Kratz
3901A S. Dixie Highway
West Palm Beach, FL 33405
561.832.8180
www.harriskratz.com

John Salibello
221 East 60th Street
New York, NY 10022
212.838.5767
www.johnsalibelloantiques.com
Fine antiques.

Kinnaman & Ramaekers
2466 Main Street
Bridgehampton, NY 11932
631.537.3838
Fine antiques.

Mondocane
174 Duane Street
New York, NY 10013
212.219.9244
www.mondomodern.com
Vintage modern furniture and
accessories.

BEDS, BEDDING AND LINENS

Leron
745 Fifth Avenue
New York, NY 10021
212.753.6700
Luxury sheets and linens custom made
in New York City.

John Robshaw
www.johnrobshaw.com
Luxury textiles and linens.

Mary Mahoney
351 Worth Avenue
Palm Beach, FL 33480
561.655.5751
Modern bedding.

Stella
138 West Broadway
New York, NY 10013
212.233.9610
Luxury linens.

Sue Fisher King
3067 Sacramento Street
San Francisco, CA
888.811.7276
www.suefisherking.com
Luxury sheeting, throws, coverlets,
and bedspreads.

CATALOGS AND CHAIN STORES

These stores are located in shopping
centers and cities nationwide—and of
course have catalogs and online stores.

Anthropologie
www.anthropologie.com
Vintage-inspired home furnishings
and fashion.

Bed Bath & Beyond
www.bedbathandbeyond.com
Linens, bedding, and housewares.

The Conran Shop
www.conranusa.com
Contemporary home furnishings and
house and cookware.

Container Store
www.containerstore.com
Everything you need to organize your
drawers, closets, kitchen, bathroom,
and den.

Crate & Barrel
www.crateandbarrel.com
Modern and affordable furniture,
tabletop, and housewares.

Design Within Reach
www.dwr.com
Modern design.

Gumps
www.gumps.com
Luxury gifts, accessories, and home
furnishings.

Horchow
www.horchow.com
Unique furniture and home décor.

IKEA
www.ikea.com
Modern, affordable furniture, tabletop,
and linens.

Pier 1 Imports
www.pier1.com
Modern and international home décor.

Pottery Barn
www.potterybarn.com
Modern and affordable furniture,
housewares, and accessories.

Restoration Hardware
www.restorationhardware.com
Vintage-inspired hardware, home
furnishings, accessories, and gifts.

Room & Board
www.roomandboard.com
Affordable contemporary furniture.

Source Perrier
www.sourceperrier.com
Unique home furnishings and
accessories.

West Elm
www.westelm.com
Modern furniture and accessories.

Wisteria
www.wisteria.com
Antique and decorative home
furnishings and accessories.

Z Gallerie
www.zgallerie.com
Modern furniture, bedding, and
accessories.

CHILDREN'S FURNITURE

Ducduc
524 Broadway, No. 206
New York, NY 10012
212.226.1868
www.ducducnyc.com
Contemporary furniture.

NettoCollection
866.996.3886
www.nettocollection.com
Stylish nursery and children's
furniture, gifts, and bedding.

DESIGN SERVICES

Charlotte Moss
20 East 63rd Street
New York, NY 10021
212.308.3888
www.charlottemoss.com
Traditional style.

Christina Murphy Interiors
666 Greenwich Street, Suite 642
New York, NY 10014
212.842.0773
www.christinamurphyinteriors.com

Emily Summers Design Associates
4639 Insurance Lane
Dallas, TX 75205
www.emilysummers.com

Kemble Interiors
294 Hibiscus Avenue
Palm Beach, FL 33480
561.659.5556

224 West 30th Street, 13th floor
New York, NY 10001
212.675.9576

www.kembleinteriors.com

Ren Interiors
Michael De Perno
2245 Cummings Drive
Santa Rosa, CA 95404
707.591.3446
reninteriors@earthlink.net
Modern and eclectic rooms.

FLEA MARKETS

http://fleamarketguide.com/
Flea Market Guide—a continuously
updated list of U.S. flea markets, state
by state.

FURNITURE

Abat Jours
44.7764.285801
www.abatjours.com
French custom lampshade maker to
the trade.

American Leather
www.americanleather.com
Fine leather furniture sold by
authorized dealers nationwide.

Am Collections
8687 Melrose Avenue, B257
West Hollywood, CA 90069
323.888.6875

540 Broadway, Suite 201
New York, NY 10012
212.625.2616

D & D Building
979 Third Avenue, Suite 1700
New York, NY 10022

www.amcollections.com
Modern furniture to the trade.

Bo Concept
888.616.3620
www.boconcept.com
Contemporary, minimalist furniture in
stores nationwide.

Charles Edwards
582 King's Road
London, England SW6 2DY
44.0.20.7736.8490
www.charlesedwards.com
Antique and reproduction lamps and
lighting fixtures.

Comerford Hennessy
2442 Main Street
Bridgehampton, NY 11932
631.537.6200
www.comerfordhennessy.com/
Modern handcrafted furniture.

David N. Ebner
5 Newey Lane
Brookhaven, New York 11719
631.286.4523
www.davidnebner.com
Modern custom furniture design.

David Sutherland Showroom
D & D Building
979 Third Avenue, Suite 813
New York, NY 10022
212.871.9717
www.davidsutherlandshowroom.com
Modern furniture to the trade.

Lamps Plus
800.782.1967
www.lampsplus.com
Online source for a variety of lighting
and fixtures.

Laneventure
P.O. Box 849
Conover, NC 28613
800.235.3558
www.laneventure.com
Manufacturer of a range of furniture
styles, including Celerie Kemble
designs, available in stores nationwide.

Oly Studio
775.336.2100
www.olystudio.com
Ultra-modern furnishings sold
nationwide.

Phurniture
8 Bond Street
New York, NY 10001
212.575.2925
www.phurniture.com
Contemporary furniture as well as
lighting. Showroom to the trade.

RUGS

ABC Carpet & Home
888 Broadway
New York, NY 10003
212.473.3000
www.abchome.com
New, vintage, and antique rugs. Also
home to Madeline Weinrib rugs.

Carini & Lang
335 Greenwich Street
New York, NY 10013
646.613.0497
www.carinilang.com
Fine hand-woven carpets.

Madeline Weinrib
ABC Carpet
888 Broadway
New York, NY 10003
212.473.3000
www.madelineweinrib.com
Contemporary, graphic rugs, pillows,
and throws.

Odegard
212.545.0069
www.odegardinc.com
Stephanie Odegard–designed rugs.

Rosemary Hallgarten
1 Simms Street, Suite 250
San Rafael, CA 94901
415.456.2588
www.rosemaryhallgarten.com
Custom-made rugs, throws, and
pillows.

Stark Carpet
979 Third Avenue
New York, NY 10022
212.752.9000
www.starkcarpet.com
Custom-designed carpets, fabric,
and furniture.

WALLPAPER & TEXTILES

Brunschwig & Fils
75 Virginia Road
North White Plains, NY 10603
914.684.5800
www.brunschwig.com
Classic, decorative wallpaper and
textiles sold at authorized dealers and
through interior designers nationwide.

Cole & Son
Chelsea Harbour Design Centre,
Ground floor 10
Lots Road
London, England SW10 0XE
0207.376.4628
www.cole-and-son.com
Fine hand-printed, block-printed, and
custom wallpapers.

Cowtan & Tout
212.647.6900
www.cowtan.com
Luxury fabrics and wall coverings sold
through interior designers and through
authorized dealers nationwide.

Bergamo Fabrics
914.665.0800
www.bergamofabrics.com
Contemporary fabrics available from
authorized dealers nationwide.

F. Schumacher
79 Madison Avenue, 15th Floor
New York, NY 10016
800.523.1200
Fine fabrics.

Holland and Sherry
979 Third Avenue, #1402
New York, NY 10017
212.355.6241
www.hollandandsherry.com
Fine fabrics.

Lee Jofa
888.533.5632
www.leejofa.com
Fine decorative and traditional fabrics
and wall coverings available through
interior designers and authorized
dealers nationwide.

Osborne & Little
203.359.1500
www.osborneandlittle.com
Fine European classic fabrics and wall
coverings available through interior
designers and authorized dealers.

Robert Kime
121-121A Kensington Church Street
London, England W8 2LP
020.7229.0886
www.robertkime.com
Contemporary and traditional English
wall coverings and fabrics.

Secondhand Rose
138 Duane Street
New York, NY 10013
212.393.9002
www.secondhandrose.com
Vintage wallpapers, linoleum, lamps,
and fixtures.

Valtekz
2125 Southend Drive, Suite 251
Charlotte, NC 28203
704.332.5277
www.valtekz.com
Composite fabrics and faux animal
skins, including the Celerie Kemble
line, sold to the trade and through
authorized dealers.

Walnut Wallpaper
7220 Beverly Boulevard, Suite 201
Los Angeles, CA 90036
323.932.9166
www.walnutwallpaper.com
Contemporary, graphic wallpapers.

Zoffany
800.894.6185
www.zoffany.com
Residential and commercial wall
coverings, both stock and custom-
made, sold through authorized dealers
nationwide.

Miscellaneous

alice + olivia
80 West 40th Street #2
New York, NY 10017
212.840.1155
www.aliceandolivia.com
Women's apparel.

Lela Rose
224 West 30th Street
New York, NY 10001
212.947.9204
www.lelarose.com
Women's apparel sold in fine stores
nationwide.

Richters of Palm Beach
224 Worth Avenue
Palm Beach, FL 33480
561.655.0774
www.worth-avenue.com/148/
Fine jewelry.

The Shoe Garden
152 West Tenth Street
New York, NY 10014
212.989.4320
www.shoegardennyc.com
Fine children's shoes.

Van Wyck & Van Wyck
224 West 30th Street
New York, NY 10012
212.675.8601
www.vanwyck.net
Event planning.

Auction Houses

The auction houses listed here offer a
wide variety of goods from all periods,
from sixteenth-century antique seating
to 1960s art pottery. The best way to
find out what they're selling is to
check their websites for current and
upcoming auctions and auction
catalogs (which can be requested
online or via telephone).

California
A.N. Abell Auction Company
2613 Yates Avenue
Commerce, CA 90040
310.858.3073
www.abell.com

Auctions by the Bay, Alameda
2700 Saratoga Street
Alameda, CA 94501
510.740.0220
www.auctionsbythebay.com

Bonham's and Butterfields
220 San Bruno Avenue
San Francisco, CA 94103
415.861.7500
www.bonhams.com

Christies Los Angeles
360 North Camden Drive
Beverly Hills, CA 90210
310.385.2644

Los Angeles Modern Auctions
1728 Laurel Canyon Boulevard
Los Angeles, CA 90046
323.904.1950
www.lamodern.com

New Jersey
Rago Arts and Auction Center
333 North Main Street
Lombertville, NJ 08530
www.ragoarts.com

New York
Christies New York
20 Rockefeller Plaza
New York, NY 10020
212.636.2000
www.christies.com

Doyle New York
175 East 87th Street
New York, NY 10128
212.427.2730
www.doylenewyork.com/default.htm

Sotheby's
1334 York Avenue
New York, NY 10021
800.813.5968
www.sothebys.com/

Stair Galleries
34 East 81st Street #1B
New York, NY 10028
212.288.1088
www.stairgalleries.com/

Tepper Galleries
110 East 25th Street
New York, NY 10010
212.677.5300
www.teppergalleries.com/

Books

There are numerous design books that
provide inspiration and information.
Below is a short list for anyone
interested, as I am, in the theory of
design and the philosophy of aesthetics.

The Architecture of Happiness, by
Alain de Botton (Pantheon, 2006)
How architecture affects our lives and
speaks to us.

Georgraphy of Home, by Akiko Busch
(Princeton Architectural Press, 2003)
Philosophy of home.

*The Substance of Style: How the Rise
of Aesthetic Value Is Remaking
Commerce, Culture, and Consciousness,* by Virginia Postrel (Harper-
Collins, 2003)
This social scientist offers compelling
arguments and insights about, and
examples of, the value of aesthetics in
contemporary society.

Many hands and minds came together to create this book. All of the rooms and design tips offered in its pages are the result of an enormously collaborative effort, and I am hugely grateful to everyone involved. First and foremost, there's no bottom to the well of love and admiration I feel toward my mom, Mimi McMakin, and her partner, Brooke Huttig, of Kemble Interiors, Palm Beach (opposite). Their style, wit, energy, and resourcefulness are my greatest inspiration. They have created and watched over (and tormented) the extended family that makes Kemble Interiors: Leslie Hardy, Leslie Gaudo, Kerol DeCristo, Lori Deeds, Kristen Fisk, Marga Zurovskis, Patti Blank, R'Lynn Allore, Heather Jones, Keithly Miller, Janet Piller, Lois Wideman, and Franco Basurto.

My New York creative team and multitasking wonders (shown at right)—Leah Forma Nichols, Charlotte Barnes, Rhea Tziros, and Sarah Connolly and now independent designers Sara Gilbane, Sarah Glisker, and Christina Murphy—have made years of crazy work and outrageous challenges a day-by-day pleasure. They have scooped and bundled—and resisted pelting me with—my scattered marbles a thousand times. I am a lucky woman to have friends with such talent, kindness, and humor working with me. Though we're a ladies-only gaggle, we all rely on the constant flexibility, resourcefulness and years of knowledge shared by the men we work with daily. Thank you to Ilan Telmont, Thomas Wu, Jeffery Edlin, Jose Escobar, Archie McAlister, and Christopher Rollinson and, from the early days, Ron Sade, Harry Spitz, and Kuni.

Love and thanks to my dad, Bill Kemble, stepmother, Julie Kemble, and my sisters, Phoebe and Madeleine, for their love and support always. I am also a lucky girl to have found my way to the Curry family, and owe special thanks to Beth for her constant thoughtfulness. For wrangling my mother and doting on our house with tender love, years of overdue and often forgotten thanks belong to my stepfather, Leroy McMakin.

Also, I owe huge thank-yous to all members of the Maddock family and to the town of Palm Beach for their continued priorities of preserving The Old Church.

I can't stop getting teary even in the attempt to express thanks to my husband, Boykin Curry. I hope he knows that, book and beyond, I just don't have a grasp of the words to thank him for all he has shared with me. I've huge hugs (and some apologies for the lost hours) for my son, Rascal, and daughter, Zinnia (whom I haven't met as of this writing, but who has been onboard for the entire project). I'm looking forward to more time with you both and all the places, because of your presence in them, that I will discover to be home too.

This book would not have been possible had it not been for my agent, Jennifer Joel; writing partner, Karen Kelly; editor, Aliza Fogelson; book coordinator, Sarah Connolly; photographer, Zach Desart; and friend, Lucia Davidson.

Finally, to all my clients, who have opened their doors, shared their creativity, and exercised patience as they have learned along with me and taught me much too. In order to protect their privacy I will not list them by name, but they know who they are. I can't thank them enough for sharing their distinct style and taste and, oftentimes, lasting friendship with me.

All photographs by Zach DeSart except the following:

Page 11, 193 (top left), 194, 219: **William Waldron**

Page 14, 17 (all of top row; second row center and right; all of third row; fourth row right and left), 19, 20 (fourth row far left and second from right), 26 (top right): **Courtesy of the Kemble family**

Page 15: **Michael Price**

Page 17 (second row far left; fourth row center): **John Haynesworth**

Page 18, 226 (top right), 229: **Carmen Schiavone**

Page 20 (top row far left; top row second from left; top row far right; second row far left; second row second from left; third row; fourth row second from left, second from right); 22-23, 228: **Noe Dewitt**

Page 25: **Fernando Bengochea**

Page 26 (top left and bottom images): **Guillermo Cawley**

Page 29 (top row left), 76, 78, 79 (top left and bottom left): **Celerie Kemble**

Page 29 (top right; second row center and right; third row center): **Michael Deperno**

Page 29 (third row left; fourth row left), 222: **Hickey-Robertson**

Page 29 (bottom right), 113 (fourth row second from left): **Travis Roozee**

Page 32, 35 (bottom): **James Wilson**

Page 35 (top right and left), 135 (top left), 136, 193 (bottom): **Michael Mundy**

Page 36–37: **Pieter Estersohn**

Page 44 (bottom), 139 (left), 146 (left), 183 (left), 241: **Annie Schlechter** courtesy of *Metropolitan Home*

Page 48 (top four), 113 (fourth row far left): **Christopher Rollinson**

Pages 54–55: Image Copyright **Alex James Bramwel**, 2007 Used under license from Shutterstock.com.

Page 56 (artwork), 77, 226 (top left): **Mimi McMakin**

Page 61 (top): **Joe Oppedisano**

Page 61 (bottom): Courtesy of **Richters of Palm Beach**

Pages 62–63: **Jeremy Liebman**

Page 73 (top and middle): Courtesy of **Lela Rose**

Page 73 (bottom), 109 (right); 110–111, 170, 220 (top right): **Francesco Lagnese**

Page 79 (bottom right), 142, 204 (left): **Nathan Coe**

Page 84-85: **Dwight Eschliman**

Page 98-99, 113 (second row far left), 125, 133, 172 (top), 183 (right), 235, 238 (top left): **Paul Costello**

Page 104 (top right and left), 239: **Christina Murphy**

Page 106: **Antonis Achilleos**

Page 114, 202 (top left), 203, 213, 216 (top): **Thomas Shelby**

Page 115, 134: **Jim Bastardo**

Page 117-120, 162, 184, 236–237: **Oberto Gili**

Page 123, 129, 135 (top right), 137, 168, 171, 172 (bottom), 188: **Don Freeman**

Page 132 (left): **Wendell Webber**

Page 150, 151: **Justin Bernhaut**

Page 161, 214: **Carlos Domenech**

Page 178 (top): **Tria Giovan**

Page 207 (top right), 242 (bottom row center): **Joe Standart**

Page 224 (top): **Lizzie Himmel**

Page 252: **Thibault Jeanson**

Page 253 (second from bottom): **Christian Grattan**

Marbleized pattern on case: **Christopher Kittrell**

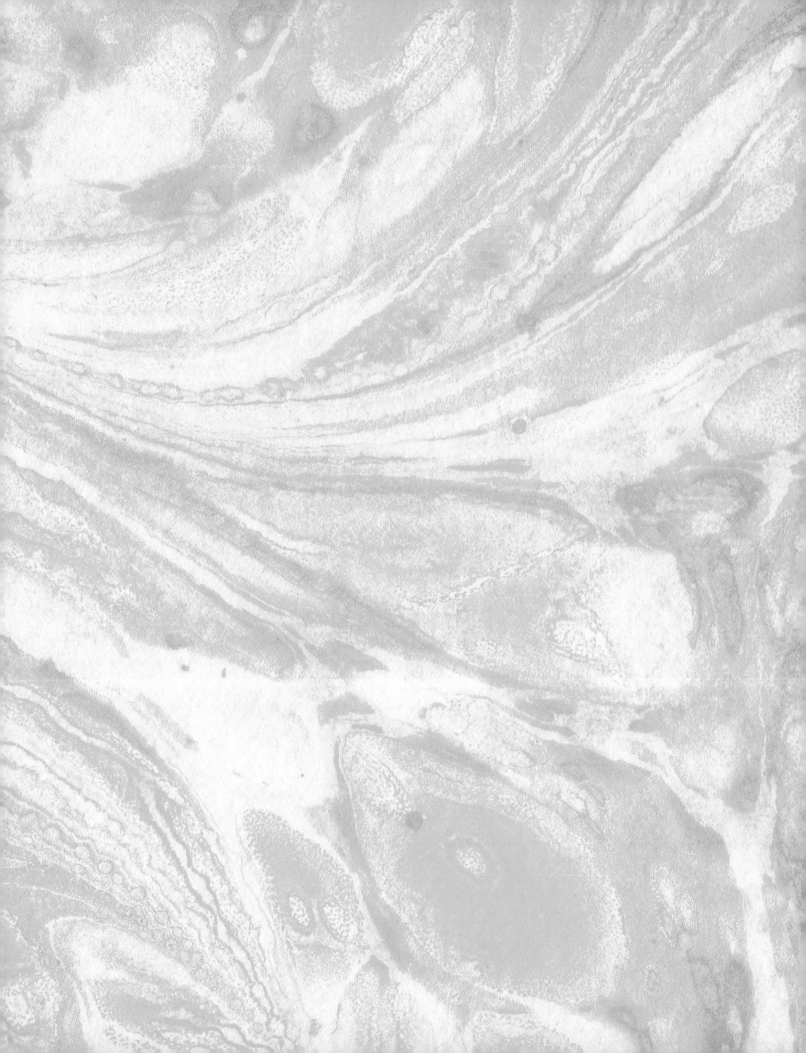